how to build

Pet Housing

by Donald R. Brann

Library of Congress Card No. 75–269

SECOND PRINTING – 1975

Published by
DIRECTIONS SIMPLIFIED, INC.

Division of
**EASI - BILD PATTERN CO., INC.
Briarcliff Manor, N.Y. 10510**

FIRST PRINTING – 1975

ISBN 0-87733-751-9

ANEBE

If you asked one or a thousand people what they most wanted out of life, the majority would answer, "Good health, financial security, peace of mind." Learning to live and work without tension, at peace with yourself and those you love, requires an ingredient we identify as ANEBE—An Ego Building Endeavor.

One's ego contains many magical properties. If we feel good we help insure good health. If we enjoy constructive activity, we do more. Anebe accentuates the positive. Building your own ego while you expand the ego of those near you, attracts love and cooperation. It helps make life worth living. Harm an ego, yours, or others, and you help destroy an individual. You won't find ANEBE in any dictionary. We coined it to describe a mental, physical and chemical reaction that develops between people or between people and the solution to a problem.

Psychologists have identified and classified many elements that attract friendship, spark a love affair, enhance one's health, even extend longevity, but relatively little is known about the chemistry that develops between people and the ego building that results from the economical solution to a costly problem.

This book simplifies building selected projects that generate Anebe for every hour invested. Try building one and you'll begin to feel feet taller. Encourage a youngster to help build and note how it creates a feeling of importance. This can trigger a lifetime interest in woodworking. I know. That's exactly how I got started when I was six years old.

Don R. Brann

TABLE OF CONTENTS

TO CREATE AN IMPORTANT INTEREST

Only a few years ago dogs were primarily household pets. Today they provide protection and no small measure of survival insurance. A well placed doghouse can help generate many nights of peaceful sleep. Parents should encourage a child to assume all responsibility for the care, feeding and housing a dog and other pets. A child should be encouraged to help build the needed shelter before purchase. Building a pet house or cage can spark a part or full time business opportunity for a teenager or retiree.

Most parents now realize the importance of guiding a youngster into areas of self sufficiency. No longer can children safely mix freely with "friends." Until a child develops into an individual with time consuming interests, he is vulnerable to "being accepted."Harness the power of a child's love for a pet and you could shape and save an individual. Only by shaping an individual at the earliest possible age can an intelligent parent expect a child to successfully survive preteen and teenage school years.

By emphasizing the need for proper feeding, grooming, regularity of body functions, the sickening results of allowing foreign matter to enter the bloodstream, you condition a child's mind to the danger of experimentation. Pet ownership also helps the parent prepare a youngster to the meaning of death.

Since all too many youngsters become joiners before they mature as an individual, encouraging them to develop a time consuming interest contains many plus benefits. Alert parents now realize being accepted and popular in today's preteen and teenage society requires drugs, sex and alcohol. While taking care of pets doesn't have the charisma of a sorority or fraternity, it offers a safer, healthier and constructive end use of free time. Remember — today's joiners are tomorrow's losers.

7

Building a doghouse, an all weather cat entry, catpartment, duck inn, rabbit hutch, kennel, parakeet or guinea pig cage, following directions outlined, offers an economical solution to needed housing. It also offers a business of your own opportunity. Because of their overall size, pet housing costs big money to ship even a short distance. Building one or each of the shelters a pet owner requests can put a youngster or retiree into business with a small investment for materials.

Doing something you have never done before, doing work that requires following simplified directions, helps expand one's sphere of activity while it helps release tension. Parents who encourage a child to help frequently trigger a lifetime interest in woodworking.

Besides simplifying construction of a plywood doghouse, directions tell how to build all the shelters illustrated. The all weather cat entry appeals to every cat owner who dislikes getting out of a warm bed on a cold night. When installed in a basement window, the cat can get in out of the weather whenever it wants.

The CATPARTMENT* has considerable potential since it can be rented to pet owners who travel. Several of these units can be placed one over one, or end to end in a garage and used as a boarding house.

Youngsters who receive baby ducks at Easter will have a chance of watching them grow in the duck inn. This practical and enchanting project contains a swimming pool plus a sand beach. It provides needed shelter while inn activities fascinate the entire family.

Construction of a rabbit hutch designed for pet or commercial use is shown on page 82. Raising rabbits for meat is developing into a sizeable and important industry. As the world food supply shrinks while the population explodes, the potential is unlimited. Learning to raise ducks, rabbits and parakeets

* TM, Reg. Directions Simplified, Inc.

provides valuable experience that can develop into a business career for those who want to be their own boss.

A private or commercial type of kennel can be constructed following directions on page 114. Directions for building a parakeet cage, page 153, plus a cage for guinea pigs (cavy), hamsters and white mice, page 172, are also included.

Provide a pet with a safe and dry shelter, one that's warm in winter, cool in summer, and you activate magnetic waves of affection. A pet can't say thanks in words, but it says plenty in sounds and motions that express approval and appreciation. A child quickly establishes a positive contact with the pet. This permits the youngster to develop responsibility, a feeling of being of service. Success in caring for a pet creates self confidence. Expand this link to a meaningful interest, and you help develop an individual.

TO HAVE FUN AND EARN EXTRA INCOME

Directions simplify building a doghouse, Illus. 1, measuring 38 x 40¼ x 46½" OD.* This can be built to any other size needed to accommodate other breeds.

①

*OD Using ¾" plywood.

An all weather cat entry, complete with a sleeping area, is shown in Illus. 2.

②

A completely enclosed catpartment, one that appeals to apartment dwellers as well as homeowners is shown in Illus. 3. It contains three separate rooms, a center sleeping area, dining area, plus a pull-out drawer litter box. Sliding doors on each side of the sleeping compartment permit feeding and/or cleaning the house while the boarder is locked into any one of three sections. The owner places the cat in the sleeping area. It is then free to move into the other rooms. When any need arises, it can be locked into the sleeping or dining area when the litter tray is removed.

Cat owners who live in apartments are prime rental customers for catpartments. They invariably get a neighbor to water and feed. The cat doesn't leave home. The apartment is kept free of litter, no stranger handles the cat and the pet isn't exposed to the disease and lack of care it might receive in a public kennel.

10

Where local codes prevent placing pet housing outdoors, regularly attended catpartments, stored in a garage, can produce a steady income. With proper care they can be maintained odor free.

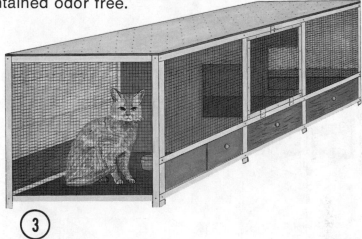

Those interested in developing a spare or full time business should talk to veterinarians, chain store managers that sell pets and/or pet supplies. Show pictures of each project. Customers who make reservations at a travel agency should be asked whether they own a pet. Prospective customers should be invited to visit your facility before they decide to board. Offer a 10% commission on every rental or sale.

The duck inn, Illus. 4, has great appeal to those who want to raise baby ducks. This contains a sand beach and swimming pool.

A single and multiple type of rabbit hutch is shown in Illus. 5.

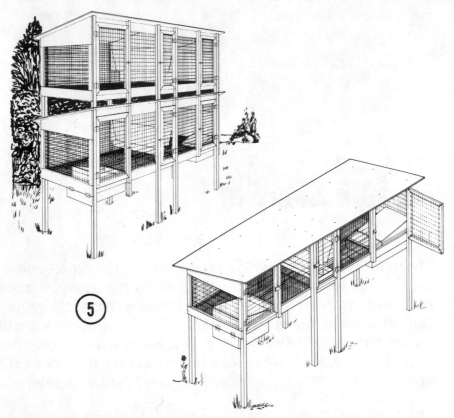

⑤

A private, or commercial style two run kennel, Illus. 6, can be built to size specified alongside a garage. It can be expanded to include as many additional units as needed. Directions for building a lean-to kennel start on page 114.

The parakeet cage, Illus. 7, provides excellent housing. Like all the other shelters, its size costs big money to pack and ship. If you build for resale, show samples to pet store managers. They will be encouraged to refer new parakeet owners to you if they earn a commission on each sale.

Illus. 8 shows a small cage that's ideal for guinea pigs, hamsters, white mice, etc. Its construction follows procedure outlined for the rabbit hutch.

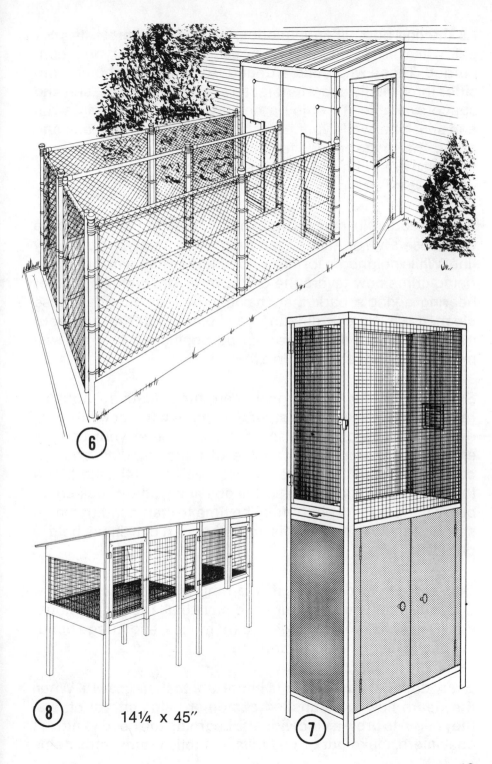

6

8   14¼ x 45"

7

13

As the dog population explodes, housing that protects your pet while he protects your house, serves everyone concerned. Those who build a doghouse or kennel should consider three vitally important factors — the neighbors, sun and space available. To enjoy a healthy life a dog needs a run and sunshine, while your neighbors are entitled to peace and quiet. The space needed for a run must provide proper drainage to an area within your property and must not contaminate your lawn or a neighbor's garden.

Zoning codes in most communities specify the distance a doghouse and/or kennel can be placed from your property line. While neighbors formerly complained about a doghouse, rising crime now favors the dog owner. Most families prefer hearing a dog's bark than having their neighbor's house cleaned out. By coordinating your plans with those of your neighbors, each doghouse can be positioned where it will protect the largest possible area.

Since a child may be allergic to hair, fur or feathers, note his reaction to a neighbor's cat, dog, canary, parakeet, rabbit or duck before purchase. Also consider whether your child is emotionally mature and capable of understanding and accepting the death of a pet. Unless you take the time and thought to condition them to this possibility, the shock could prove unnecessarily harmful. The time to start conditioning a sensitive child's mind to this important part of living is before purchase.

Only agree to its purchase if he promises to assume full care. Only buy after you and your child have built the proper housing. If the child is old enough to earn money, encourage building one each of the other projects.

Every dollar children earn is important to their growth. When they learn how one satisfied customer helps attract others, they begin to grow as individuals. Learning the need to attract customers, make out or pay bills, establish rates, etc., helps

14

develop an appreciation of time, space, money and people regardless of race, color or appearance.

Those interested in selling or renting pet shelters, or in boarding, should consider these facts. Pet owners are a special breed who relate to their pets like people should relate to people. Many take more interest in their pets than their neighbors take in their children. Because of this, building shelters and/or boarding pets can be both profitable and pleasing.

Retirees can develop an income producing part or full time business building each of these projects. When samples or photos are shown to managers of pet departments in chain stores, or where conditions permit, being displayed with a "For Sale" sign on a front lawn, it usually stops enough people to generate profitable sales. Many lumber, hardware and pet stores will buy for resale.

Those who don't have space to display samples can create interest and sales using photos of each project. When all materials are purchased locally, savings up to 75% of a retail selling price can frequently be effected.

Where a shortage of clean, disease free cat and dog boarding facilities exist, or you know one or more travel agents, or pet owners who travel, turning spare space in a garage into cat-partments, or a kennel, or building one alongside a garage wall, provides a sensible way to test potential. But first show as many potential customers, every retailer who sells pets or supplies, lumber and hardware retailers, travel agents, etc., pictures of each project.

A boarding clientele can be developed by telephone solicitation or direct mail. Drop a mimeographed announcement into the mail boxes of every home with a cat. Ask each pet owner if they know others who might be interested. Ask a friendly veterinarian to drop an announcement into his monthly statements. Ask your local savings bank and savings and loan association to help you "save more money" by dropping an announcement into their monthly statements. Ask real estate agents to offer "rentals for your catpartments." Offer a 10% commission to all who make sales or rentals. Encouraging a child to think "business" provides a valuable lesson in "growing up."

Before talking to even your first potential customer, make personal calls to learn how much local and nearby kennels charge to board a dog or cat per day, week and month. Since most pet store owners have established "kennel" connections, they will naturally try to discourage competition if you reveal your plans. Compare the going rate with the cost of food, kitty litter, etc., plus the time required to remove contents from a dropping tray, and you begin to see how a profitable business can be developed.

Measuring 24 x 24 x 48", the catpartment offers each guest complete privacy. When constructed as shown, it can be completely disinfected in minutes. Mention the all-aluminum, germ-free cleanliness of your housing units, and how aluminum simplifies disinfecting, when you talk to a prospective customer.

While everyone who follows the step-by-step directions can build the shelters, many pet owners don't have the time or inclination. This is especially true among apartment dwellers. And few cat owners living in an apartment have space to store a catpartment. Most prefer to rent when needed. Getting a neighbor to feed the pet in their apartment, while they travel, not only provides an economical solution to a costly problem but also eliminates worry about "the loved one."

TO BUILD A DOGHOUSE

The cutting chart, Illus. 9, permits building a doghouse, Illus. 10, that measures 38 x 40¼ x 46½". The 18 x 12" opening in K and L, Illus. 16, 18, is suitable for many medium size breeds, but is too small for the larger German Shepherd, Doberman, etc. To build a larger house, one that will comfortably accommodate a police dog or large collie, etc., add 6", or amount needed, to the height of K, H, D and E, 2" or more to the width. Eliminate the windbreak panel L, Illus. 18.

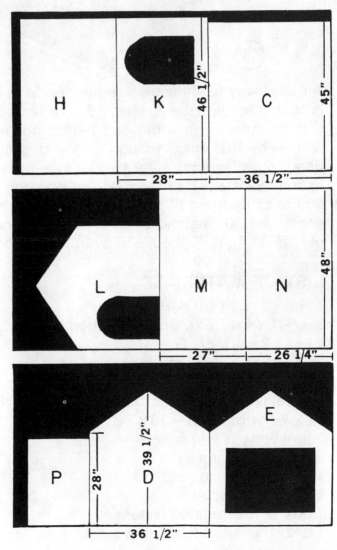

4 × 8 exterior grade plywood

⑨

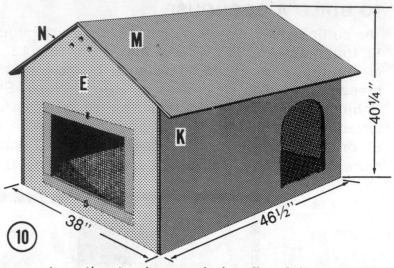

An easy way to estimate size needed to fit a full grown dog is to dummy up side K, Illus. 16. Use flat corrugated board. Cut an opening to width and height needed. The opening should be just large enough so the dog merely lowers his head to go through. Alter overall size of sides and ends to accommodate the revised size of opening. For example, if you raise opening 2″ to 20 x 12″, sides K, H and ends D, E, should be 30″ instead of 28″. The following materials simplify building a doghouse to overall size shown, Illus. 10.

LIST OF MATERIALS

1 — 2 x 3″ x 14′ for A, B
3 — ¾″ x 4 x 8′ Ext. Grade Plywood — C, D, E, H, K, L, M, N, P
1 — 1 x 2 x 6′ for F, G
24 sq. ft. of aluminum roofing and nails
1 — 1 x 3 x 8′ — screen frame optional
5 lineal feet ¾″ quarter round molding
½ x ½″ wire mesh — 18 x 24″
2 turn buttons and screws
8 penny common nails
4 penny finishing nails
½″ screen staples
1 box ⅝″ corrugated fasteners
1 doz. 1¼″ No. 8 flathead wood screws

18

If you increase the height of K, H, D and E from 28 to 34", you can cut an opening 24 x 18". If you live in an area where temperature drops sharply, and the windbreak is desired, lengthen A, C, H and K so both entry and sleeping area provide sufficient space. Consider shoulder height of your dog and cut opening in L equal to opening in K. When building for resale, ask the owner to measure shoulder height of his full grown dog. The following are average shoulder heights:

Airedale — 23"
American Cockers — 15 to 15½"
Beagle — under 13, up to 15"
Boxers — 22 to 24"
Collie — 22 to 24"
Dalmatian — 20 to 23"
Doberman — 25"
Fox Terrier — 15 to 15½"
German Shepherd — 22 to 26"
Great Dane — 28 to 30"
Newfoundland — 26 to 28"
Old English Sheepdog — 22"
Poodle — toy — up to 10"
Poodle — miniature — 10 to 14"
Poodle — standard — 15 to 16"
Retriever — 22 to 25"
Russian Wolfhound — 28 to 31"
Saint Bernard — 25 to 27½"
Scottish Terrier — 10"
Sheltie — 13 to 16"

Dimensions shown, Illus. 11, 12, 13, permit construction of a doghouse using ¾" plywood. ⅝, ½, ⅜ or ¼" plywood can be substituted. When ¼ or ⅜" is used, nail 1 x 2 nailors in position shown, Illus. 14. Exterior plywood is recommended. If exterior is too costly, use sheathing plywood. After cutting part to exact size required, paint edges and surfaces with two coats of exterior paint before assembling in position.

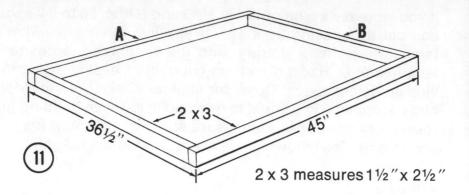

11

2 x 3 measures 1½" x 2½"

Build base, Illus. 11, using 2 x 3. Cut A — 45", B — 33½". Nail in position shown using 10 penny nails.

Cut floor C, 36½ x 45", Illus. 12, from ¼" hardboard or ⅜" plywood. Paint both faces and edge of C with wood preservative. When dry, nail C to AB with 8 penny nails.

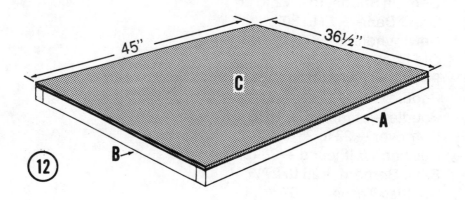

12

Cut ends D and E, Illus. 13, 36½ x 39½".

If ¼ or ⅜" plywood is used for E, D, H, K and L, nail 1 x 2 nailors to inside face of D and E, Illus. 14. Cut end E same size as D. The opening for screen, Illus. 13, is optional. If one is desired, make frame, Illus. 22, to size indicated, or size required. Draw outline of screen frame on E and cut opening to size required. If you drill a series of ⅛" holes, to start saw blade, you can save the cutout and use it as a winter panel, P, Illus. 23.

20

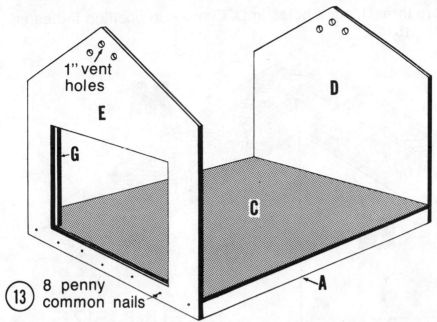

1" vent holes

E

G

D

C

8 penny common nails

A

Cut two 1 x 2 vertical screen stops G to length opening re-quires, Illus. 13; one 1 x 2 horizontal screen stop F. This is fastened across top of opening. Using 1¼" No. 8 flathead wood screws, fasten E to F and G. Allow F and G to project ⅜" into opening. This provides a shoulder for the screen or winter panel.

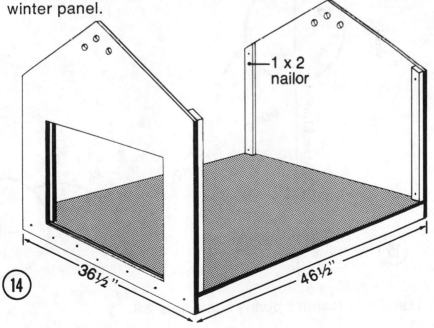

1 x 2 nailor

36½"

46½"

14

Bore three 1″ vent holes in D, E and L in position indicated, Illus. 15, 18.

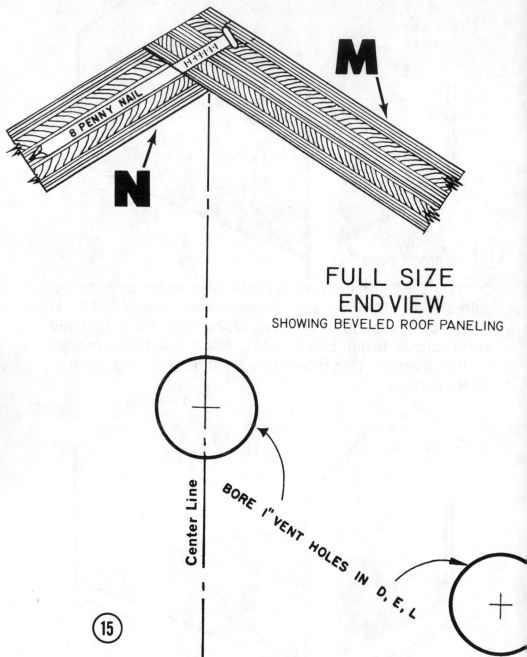

M

N

8 PENNY NAIL

FULL SIZE
END VIEW
SHOWING BEVELED ROOF PANELING

Center Line

BORE I″ VENT HOLES IN D, E, L

⑮

Nail D and E to B with 8 penny nails, Illus. 13.

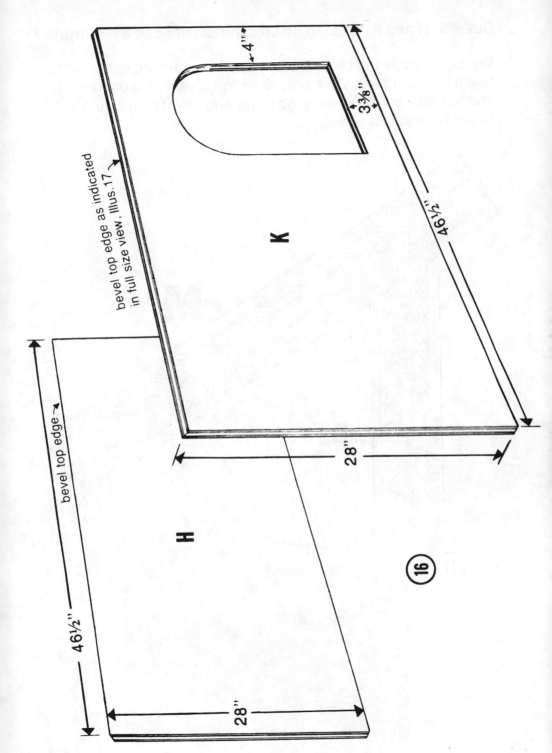

bevel top edge as indicated
in full size view, Illus. 17

4"

3⅜"

46½"

K

bevel top edge

46½"

H

28"

28"

⑯

23

Cut side H and K, Illus. 16, to size indicated or size required.

Bevel top edge of H and K to angle shown full size, Illus. 17. Use a plane or saw. When ¼ , ⅜ or ½″ plywood is used for H and K, nail 1 x 2 flush with top edge and bevel plane the 1 x 2 to angle required.

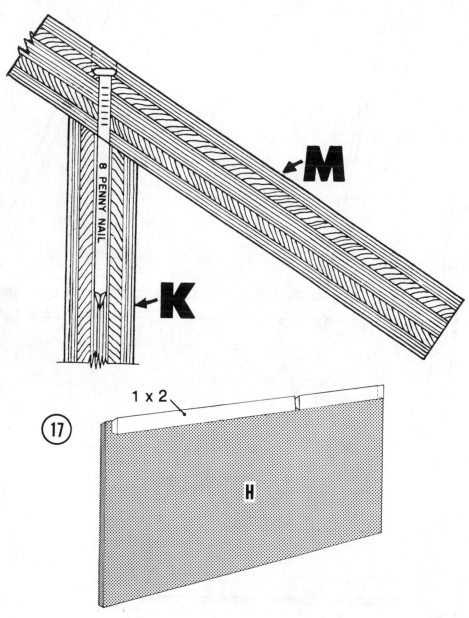

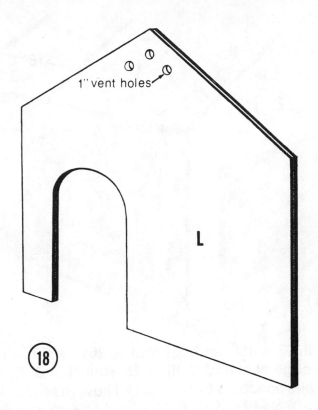

1" vent holes

L

(18)

Windbreak L, Illus. 18, is optional. If 'desired, cut to width of D and E and to height required. L is placed on top of C, Illus. 19.

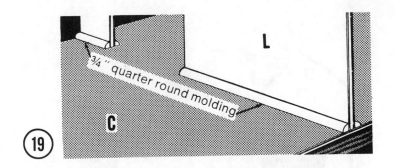

L

3/4" quarter round molding

C

(19)

Nail H and K to D, E and A, Illus. 20. Place L in position. Nail 3/4" quarter round molding in position noted, Illus. 19, to both sides of L with 4 penny finishing nails. Nail H and K to L with 6 penny nails.

25

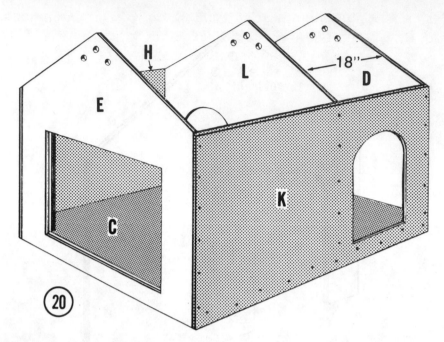

Cut roof M, 27 x 48″, and cut roof N, 26¼ x 48″, Illus. 9, 10. Bevel top edge of M and N, Illus. 15. Nail N to D, E, H, L with 8 penny nails spaced 8 to 10″ apart. N overhangs D and E by ¾″, Illus. 10. Nail M to D, E, K, L and N with 8 penny nails.

Using nailset, countersink all nails. Fill holes with putty or a woodfiller. Paint doghouse with at least two coats of exterior paint.

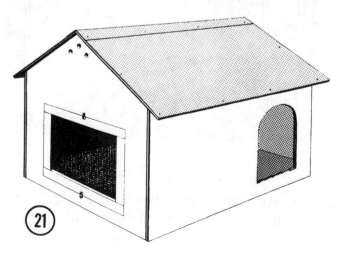

Nail sheet aluminum to roof using ⅝ or ¾″ aluminum nails. Cut an 8″ strip of aluminum to length of ridge. Bend at 4″ to cover ridge. Nail in position indicated, Illus. 21.

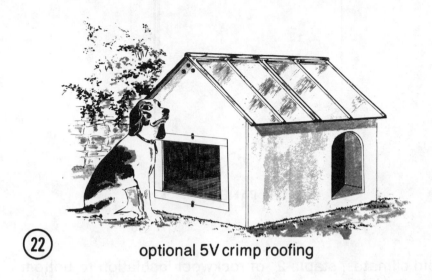

㉒   optional 5V crimp roofing

The screen, Illus. 22, or winter panel, Illus. 23, can be secured in place with two turn buttons.

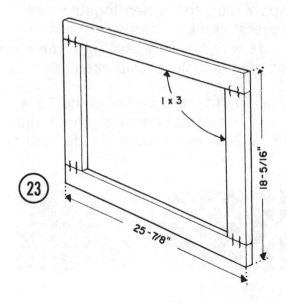

㉓

1 x 3

18-5/16″

25-7/8″

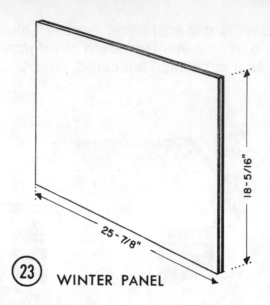

23 WINTER PANEL

18 - 5/16"

25 - 7/8"

In cold climates, staple 2″ of rockwool insulation to bottom face of C. Nail a tempered hardboard panel to A, B to hold insulation permanently in position. Place house on bricks or blocks to prevent direct contact with the earth.

The summer screen, Illus. 22, should be built from 1 x 3 to size required. Apply glue and fasten together with two ⅝″ corrugated fasteners at each corner. Check frame with square. Hold square with 1 x 2 braces. Turn frame over and drive a single corrugated fastener into each joint.

Place frame in opening to make certain it fits. ½ x ½″ wire mesh, 17 x 24″, or decorative aluminum sheet, Illus. 24, or web pattern, Illus. 25, can be nailed to inside face of frame.

28

ALL WEATHER CAT ENTRY

(26)

Everyone who owns a cat appreciates the convenience of this all weather entry, Illus. 2, 26. The "in house" door on the end or back of the shelter, Illus. 27, is kept fastened. It is opened when you want to take the cat out of the shelter. This door can be "screened" in summer. A solid panel can be inserted during the cold weather. Like the doghouse, the all weather cat entry has considerable appeal. It allows the cat to come and go at its discretion with no one having to get out of a warm bed and unlock an outside door in the dead of night. Installation requires removing one pane of glass from a basement window. A frame, Illus. 29, built to size opening requires, replaces the pane of glass. The frame permits hinging a swinging door. The entry, with shelter attached, offers a warm, dry, out of the weather housing unit the year round.

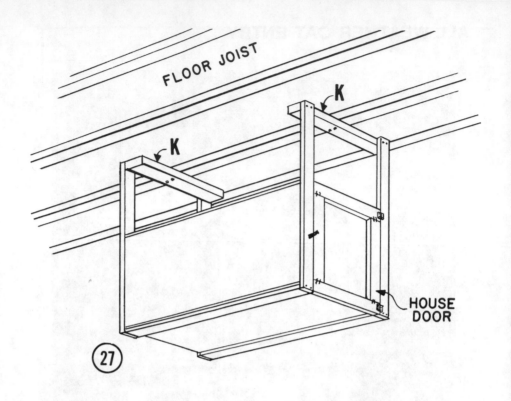

FLOOR JOIST

K

K

HOUSE
DOOR

(27)

If you want to remove a steel basement window, you can cut
a piece of ¾″ plywood to overall size of window removed. The
opening for a swinging door is cut in one side. The door is
hinged in position shown, Illus. 29, and the entire panel is then
bolted to the frame.

LIST OF MATERIALS

1 — ½ x 4 x 6′ sheathing grade plywood — A, B, C, D, E, F
1 x 2 — G, H, L, M
2 x 4 x 6′ for J or 3′ for K
4, 8 and 16 penny nails
12 — ½ x 1″ corrugated fasteners
1 — 1¾″ turn button
2 — 1½″ cabinet hinges
12 x 16″ screen cloth
¾″ Exterior Grade Plywood for N

Cut all parts to size indicated in cutting chart, Illus. 28.

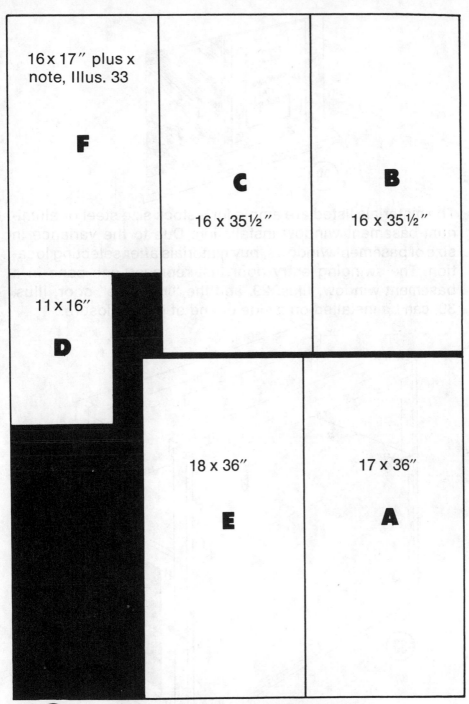

16 x 17″ plus x
note, Illus. 33

F

C

16 x 35½″

B

16 x 35½″

11 x 16″

D

18 x 36″

E

17 x 36″

A

(28) **CUTTING DIAGRAM**

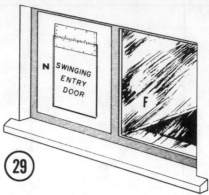

(29)

The materials listed are ample for a stock size steel or aluminum basement window installation. Due to the variance in size of basement windows, buy materials after selecting location. The swinging entry door that replaces one pane in a basement window, Illus. 29, and the "in house" door, Illus. 30, can be installed on a side or end of the enclosure.

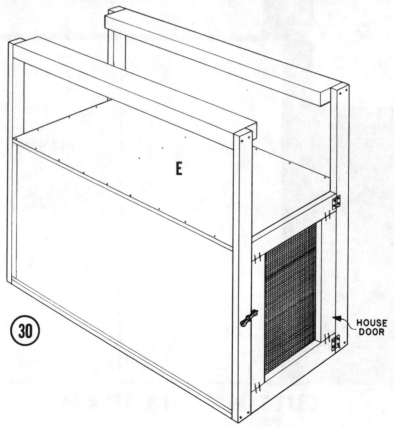

(30)

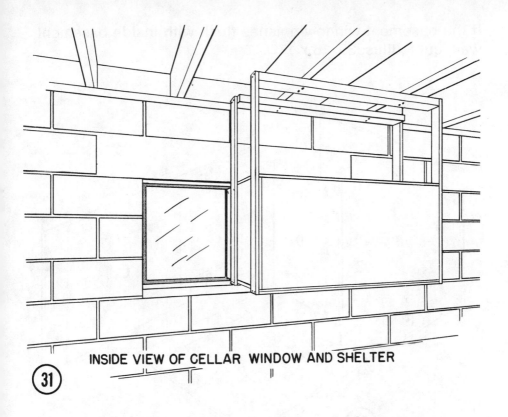

INSIDE VIEW OF CELLAR WINDOW AND SHELTER

(31)

Illus. 31 shows a typical basement installation with the shelter fastened to ceiling joists. One pane of glass in the basement window remains while one is replaced with a wood frame, Illus. 32, and a swinging door, Illus. 29.

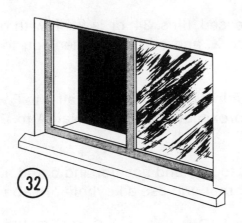

(32)

If the basement window finishes flush with inside basement wall, cut F, Illus. 33, 16 x 17".

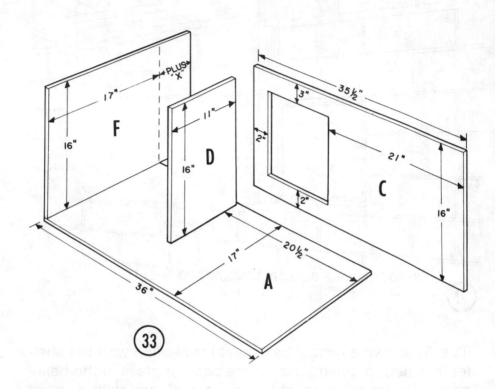

If window is recessed, Illus. 34, or is flush with outside wall, measure distance X, and add this dimension to width of F, Illus. 33.

Apply glue to all joints before nailing. Nail A to F with 4 penny nails spaced approximately 6" apart. Nail A to D in position indicated, Illus. 33.

Cut opening in C to size and position indicated. Drill a series of 1/8" holes in corner and use a keyhole or saber saw.

Glue and nail A to B, C, D, F; F to B, C; C to D; Illus. 35.

34

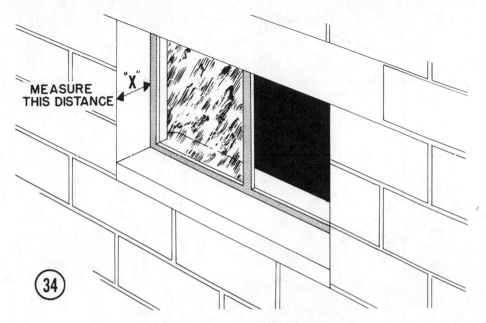

MEASURE
THIS DISTANCE

"X"

(34)

INSIDE VIEW OF CELLAR WINDOW

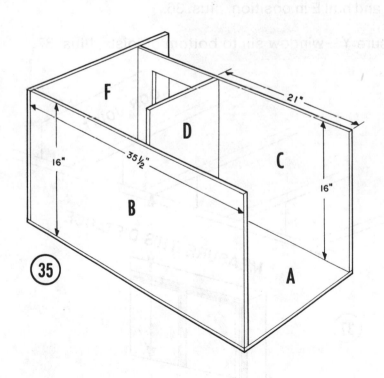

F

D

C

16"

35½"

16"

B

A

(35)

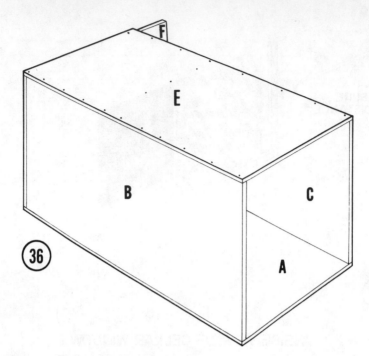

Glue and nail E in position, Illus. 36.

Measure Y—window sill to bottom of joists, Illus. 37.

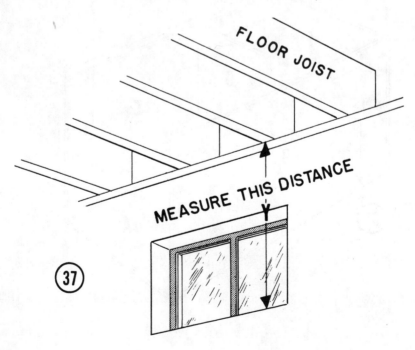

FLOOR JOIST

MEASURE THIS DISTANCE

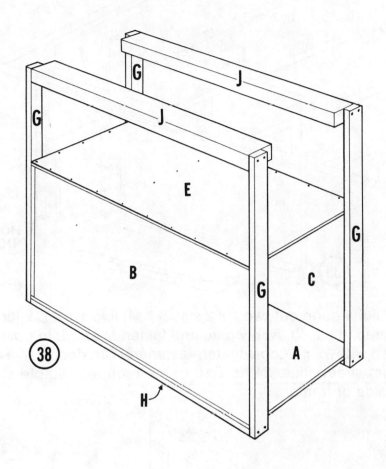

Cut four 1 x 2G, Illus. 38, to length of Y, plus ¾". Cut two
1 x 2 x 36" H. Apply glue and nail G to H; nail through H into
AB and C, using 6 penny nails.

If joists run in direction shown, Illus. 39, cut two J — 2 x 4 x 36".

If joists run in direction shown, Illus. 26, cut two K — 2 x 4 x 18".

Nail through J or K into joists with 16 penny common nails.

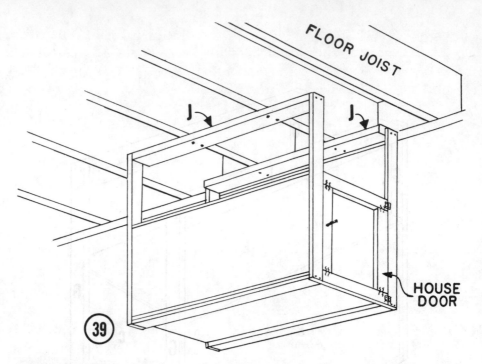

FLOOR JOIST

J

J

HOUSE
DOOR

(39)

To build a door, cut two 1 x 2 x 13⅝" M; two 1 x 2 L x length required, Illus. 40. Apply glue and fasten M and L in position shown with ½ x 1" corrugated fasteners. Cut decorative aluminum sheet, Illus. 24, to size frame requires. Staple sheet to inside of frame.

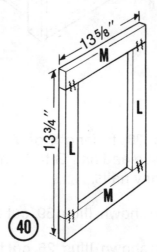

13⅝"

M

13¾"

L

L

M

(40)

Fasten two 1½" cabinet door hinges in position shown, Illus. 30. Door can be locked with turn button as indicated.

Remove one pane of glass in basement window frame, Illus. 32. Cut ⅜ or ½″ exterior plywood N, Illus. 41, to overall size of pane removed. Remove all putty. Drill four holes through N and frame and bolt or "Pop" Rivet N in position. To simplify removing pane and fastening N in position, remove sash from frame.

Cut opening, Illus. 42, 5½ x 8″. If necessary, the cutout can be used as a swinging door. Sandpaper edge so it swings freely.

When making an installation in a wood window frame, N can be nailed with 6 penny finishing nails.

If you cut N and swinging panel door from ⅜ or ½″ plywood, you can make a swinging door hinge from two 4 x 5½″ pieces of canvas, Illus. 43. Sew together through middle, Illus. 44.

Glue and staple canvas to door, Illus. 45, and to N, Illus. 29.

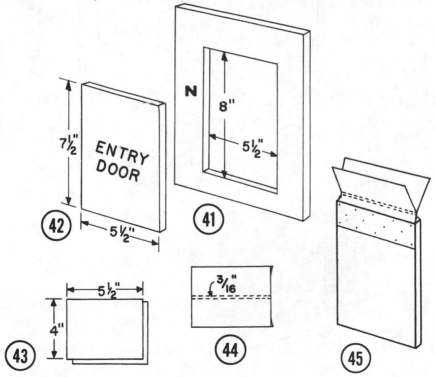

Position shelter, Illus. 31. Edge of F should butt against frame. Nail G to J (or K), Illus. 38, 46. Place food in house at the next meal time. Push cat through entry door. After two or three feedings you will again be enjoying nights of peaceful sleep.

An alternate installation can be made by removing a steel or aluminum window. Cut plywood to exact overall size of opening. Cut opening in panel, Illus. 47, Bolt panel to frame.

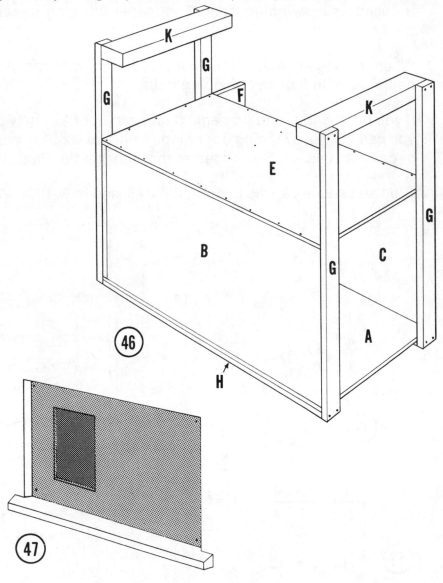

THE CATPARTMENT

As every cat owner soon learns, finding a clean, disease free, even moderately priced boarding house for a cat, before leaving on an extended trip, is no easy problem to solve. Not only do kennels charge big money, but the facilities are frequently less than desirable. The catpartment, Illus. 3, was designed to keep friends still friends while they feed and care for your pet without handling.

Designed to provide both freedom of movement and privacy, its 24 x 24 x 48" size offers ample room. Build a sample. Offer to build or rent these units and you will find immediate acceptance in most neighborhoods where owners go on vacation or travel.

The catpartment contains more space than you normally get when you board a cat at the highest priced kennels. Allow the cat to use the catpartment days before you leave. This helps alleviate the pain of departure. Ask a friend to feed while you are away, or move the unit to a friend's place. Doors permit feeding and watering. Sliding doors on both sides of the sleeping compartment permit locking the cat in the dining or sleeping area while dumping the litter drawer. Knowing your loved one is in a warm, dry and safe place helps you enjoy your trip.

Since many diseases are transmitted from one cat to another, building the shelter from aluminum permits disinfecting after each rental, and keeping it practically germ free before the next occupant moves in. Buy a strong disinfectant at your pet supply store. Use it regularly. This not only eliminates antagonistic body odors a previous visitor might have left, but also helps keep it germ free. If you build for rental, make leasing arrangements through a pet supply store, veterinarian, or travel agency. Ask your "renting agent" to tell all tenants to bring their own bedding. This keeps "tenants" much happier.

The front panel is hinged, Illus. 84. This permits owner to place pet in sleeping area with no need for a stranger to handle a boarder.

Show travel agents an 8 x 10 photograph of the catpartment. Always be prepared to leave a photo if they request one. Offer to rebate a 10% commission on the gross received from each boarder. Be sure to mention the practically germ free construction of your boarding house.

Those planning to board can stack units one over one and end to end. Before stacking, cover the top with a ¼ or ⅜" plywood panel cut to overall size of unit, plus 4" in length and width. Cover this with polyethelyne before placing next unit.

When placing units end to end or back to back, insert ⅛ or ¼" hardboard or plywood panel between units. This provides each occupant with the extra privacy it really appreciates.

LIST OF MATERIALS
1 — ⅜" x 4 x 8' plywood
1 — 36 x 36" aluminum sheet
1 — ⅛ x 24 x 48" pegboard
12 — ⅛ x ¾" x 6' bar stock
12 — ¹⁄₁₆ x 1 x 1" x 6' angle
1 — ⅝" x 2 x 2' plywood or particle board
½ x ½" plastic coated or galvanized wire — 8 lineal ft. 48" w.
4 lineal ft. — ¼" single track, or storm window extrusion
3 lineal ft. — ⅛ or ¼" sliding door track
2 — 2" drawer knobs

Always consider yourself facing the completed catpartment when noting location of any framing member.

If ¹⁄₁₆ x 1 x 1" angle isn't readily available, but ⅛ x 1 x 1" angle is, cut inner framing members to overall length required. Cut notch in AB to depth required.

Cut one bottom A — ⅜ x 23¾ x 47¾", Illus. 48.

42

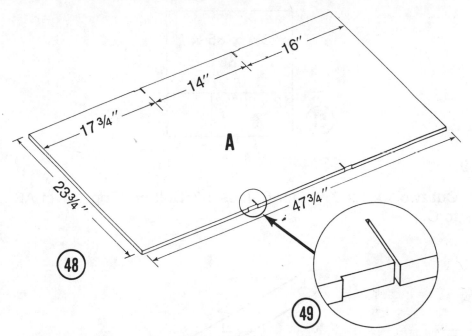

A

17 ¾″ 14″ 16″

23¾″

47¾″

(48)

(49)

Saw 1″ slots in position required to receive legs. Use a short piece of 1 x 1 x ¹⁄₁₆″ aluminum angle to test depth of each notch, Illus. 49.

Cover floor with sheet aluminum B, Illus. 50. Cut one piece 23¾ x 36″, the other 11¾ x 23¾″ from a 36 x 36″ panel, Illus. 51. Notch B where legs require same.

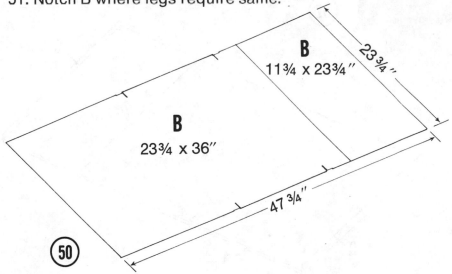

B
11¾ x 23¾″

23¾″

B
23¾ x 36″

47¾″

(50)

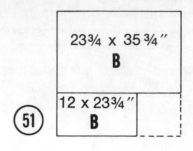

51

23¾ x 35¾"
B

12 x 23¾"
B

Cut two 1 x 1 x 23¾" for C, Illus. 52. Bolt or "Pop" Rivet AB to C.

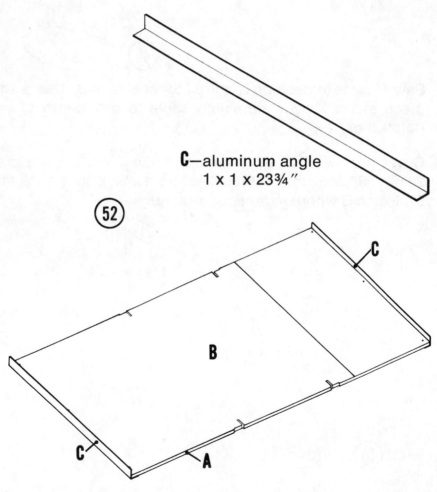

C—aluminum angle
1 x 1 x 23¾"

52

C

B

C

A

The "Pop" Rivet gun, Illus. 53, is an ingenious device. You first drill a hole to size rivet requires. Use length rivet needed to go clear through C, A and B, Illus. 54. These rivets simplify fastening aluminum to plywood, aluminum angle to angle, to pegboard, or to bar stock. Press handle and you make like a pro. If you make a mistake, drill through rivet, remove and try again.

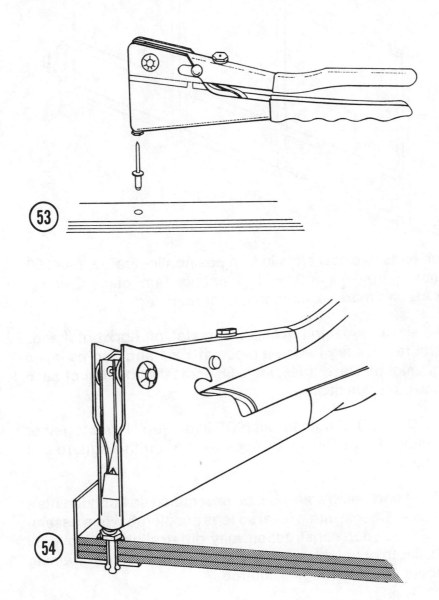

Assemble front frame, Illus. 55. Cut three 1 x 1 x 48″ aluminum angle for D, E.

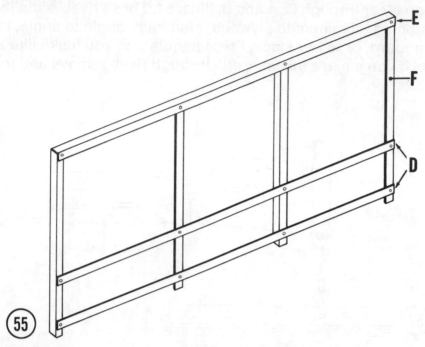

(55)

Notch ends and saw slots in D in position indicated, Illus. 56. To make sure slots in D are in exact position, place D alongside AB and mark exact location for each leg.

Saw a sliver, equal to thickness of metal, off horizontal ends of D, to receive leg F. Use a piece of 1 x 1 angle to estimate exact amount. Dash lines, Illus. 56, indicate position of each leg and direction of slot.

Clamp D to F. Drill hole through DF and "Pop" Rivet together in position shown, Illus. 55. Check each leg with a square and fasten E to F.

The front and rear frame must be assembled so each leg fits a notch in A. Check with a level so legs are plumb when assembled. Since your construction may differ slightly in overall width, depth or height, always measure and cut inner framing members to exact length required.

46

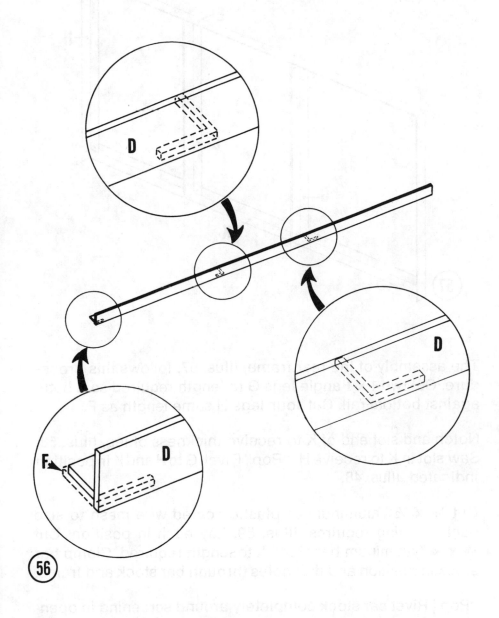

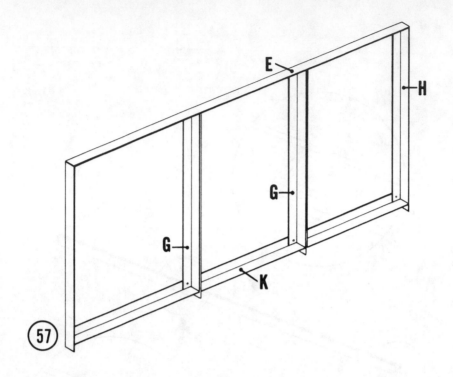

The assembly of the rear frame, Illus. 57, follows this procedure. Cut two 1 x 1 angle legs G to length required so it butts against bottom rail. Cut four legs H same length as F.

Notch and slot end of K to receive thickness of leg, Illus. 58. Saw slot in K to receive H. "Pop" Rivet G to H and K in position indicated, Illus. 48.

Cut ½ x ½" aluminum or plastic coated wire mesh to size each opening requires, Illus. 59. Lay each in position. Cut ⅛ x ¾" aluminum bar stock L to length required. Clamp bar stock in position and drill holes through bar stock and frame.

"Pop" Rivet bar stock completely around screening in opening 1.

"Pop" Rivet 1 x 1 angle M in position shown over mesh in opening 2, Illus. 59.

48

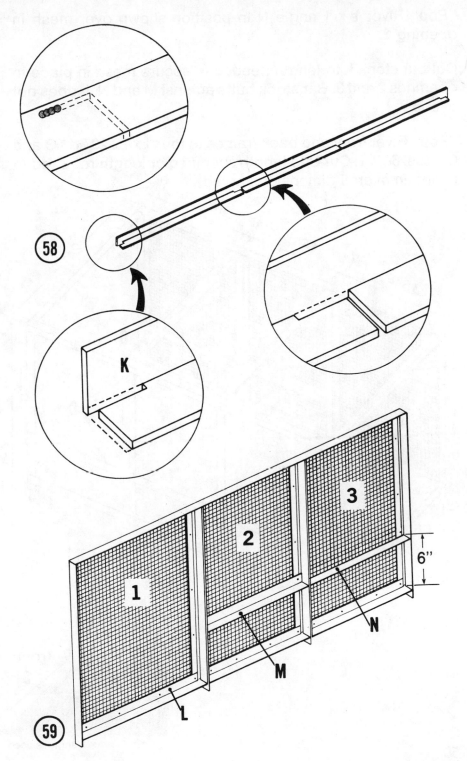

⑤⑧

K

⑤⑨

1

2

3

6"

N

M

L

"Pop" Rivet 1 x 1 angle N in position shown over mesh in opening 3.

Cut bar stock L to length needed to secure mesh in place in openings 2 and 3. Bar stock butts against M and N. it does not overlap.

"Pop" Rivet front and back frames to four 1 x 1 x 23⅞"* O and C. Illus. 60, 61. Cut O to length specified or length required to maintain overall dimensions noted.

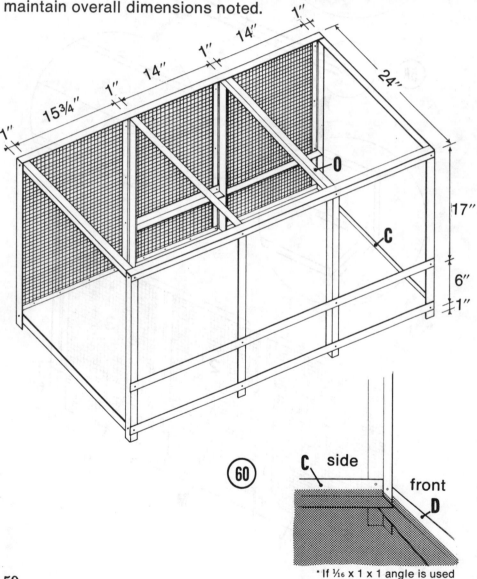

* If 1/16 x 1 x 1 angle is used

Cut two plywood spacers, ⅝ x1″ x length required, Illus. 61, 62, 63. Place spacers in position alongside legs. Drill hole through front and back rail. Fasten spacer in position by driving a 1″ aluminum nail through rail into end of spacer. Always use aluminum nails and "Pop" Rivets with aluminum framing.

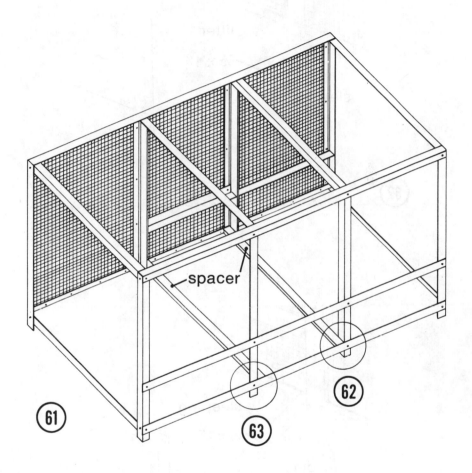

spacer

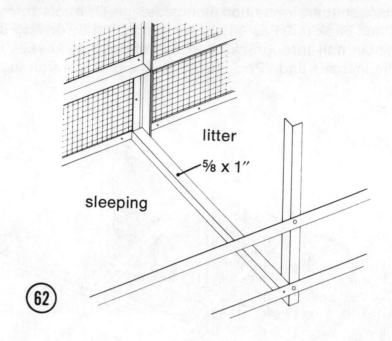

litter

⅝ x 1"

sleeping

62

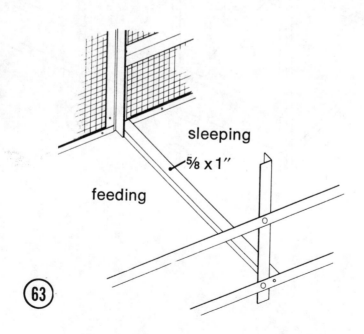

sleeping

⅝ x 1"

feeding

63

Cut aluminum or plastic coated wire mesh for end frames to size each requires. Notch ends of ⅝ x 2″ spacer, Illus. 64, to receive legs. Staple wire to edge of spacer. Drive nail through rail and C into sides of spacer in litter end, Illus. 65.

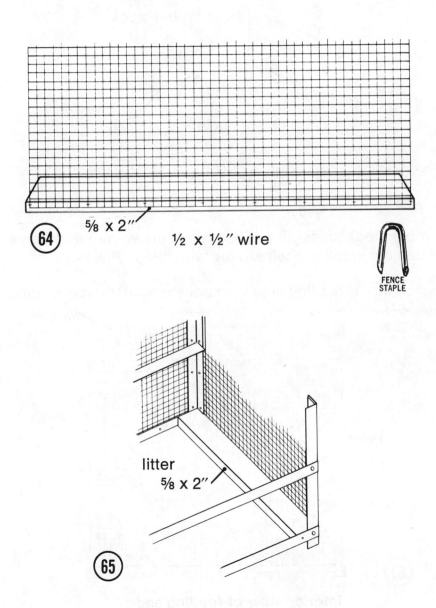

⑥④　⅝ x 2‴　　½ x ½″ wire

FENCE
STAPLE

litter
⅝ x 2″

⑥⑤

Cut a ¾ x 5″ plywood filler P, Illus. 66, so it's flush with top track. P prevents litter from filling area between track and screened end. Fasten in position with 1″ aluminum nails through FH. Cover top edge with a strip of aluminum bar stock.

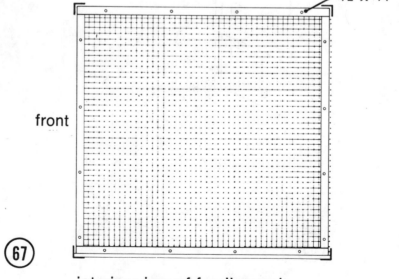

⅛ x ¾″ bar stock

P

F

66

Cut bar stock to length needed to secure wire to end frame. Fasten bar stock and wire to leg with "Pop" Rivets.

Fasten wire in feeding area with bar stock all the way around, Illus. 67.

½ x ¾″

front

67

interior view of feeding end

Fasten 1 x 1 x 23¾″ aluminum angle in position shown to both sides, top and bottom for grooming tool drawer, Illus. 68. Drill and countersink holes to receive aluminum screws, Illus. 69, 70.

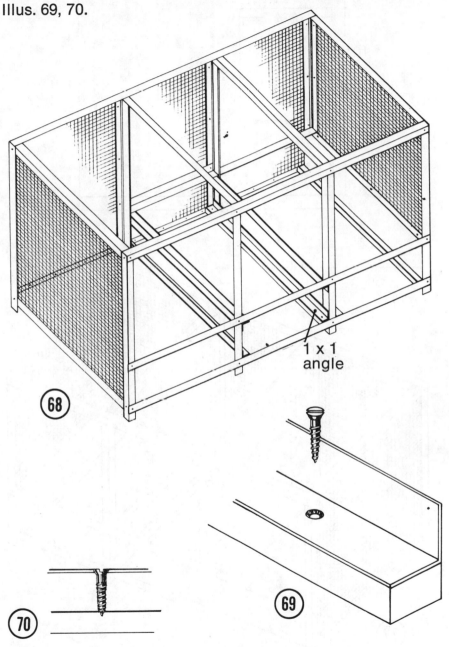

1 x 1 angle

68

69

70

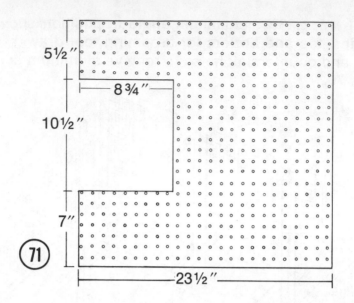

5½"

8¾"

10½"

7"

23½"

⑦⑦71

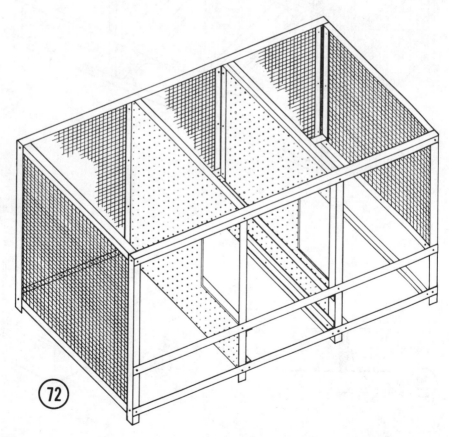

⑦72

Cut ⅛" pegboard to shape and size shown, Illus. 71, or to size required. "Pop" Rivet in position to both sides of sleeping area, Illus. 72.

Cut another ⅝ x 1" spacer x length needed. Fasten in position to left side of litter drawer area, Illus. 73. Cut four lengths of 1 x 1 x 23¾" angle. Fasten in position in litter area, Illus. 74, 75. This provides track for litter drawer.

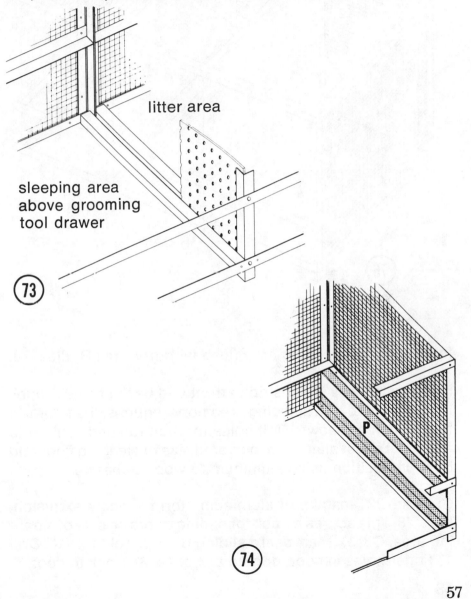

litter area

sleeping area
above grooming
tool drawer

73

P

74

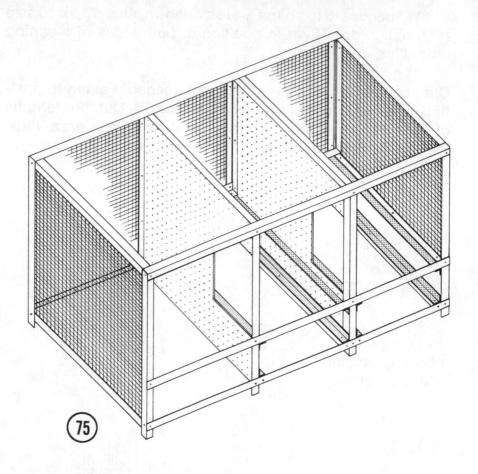

(75)

Install floor in sleeping area flush with front rail D, Illus. 76.

If you fasten a ⅝" filler strip to front and back of a ⅜" panel, Illus. 77, cut to size sleeping area floor requires, the floor will finish flush as shown. Drill holes through rail and nail rail to floor. Cut sheet aluminum to overall size of sleeping floor and bond in position using aluminum to wood adhesive.

Cut four 22" lengths of aluminum storm window extrusion, Illus. 78. This acts as a track for sliding doors on side of sleeping area. Cut ⅛" hardboard sliding door panel 11 x 11". Drill 1" finger holes in door, or glue a ¾ x 1 x 3" block to door.

58

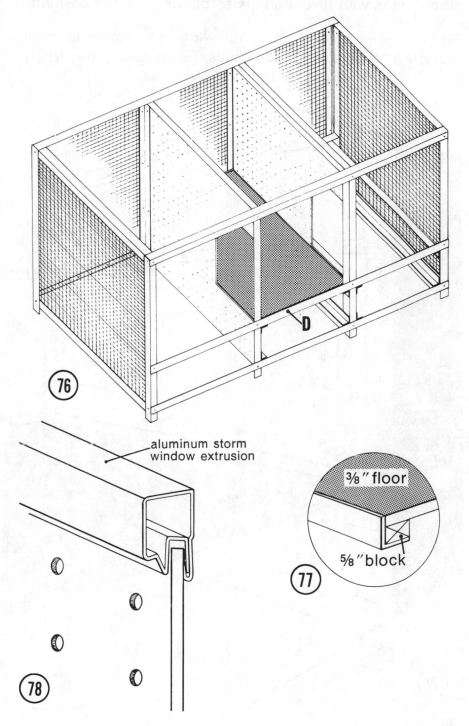

D

⑦⑥

aluminum storm
window extrusion

⅜" floor

⅝" block

⑦⑦

⑦⑧

59

Recess end of track ⅜″ from face of D. This acts as a door stop. Check with level and fasten bottom track in position.

Place door in bottom track. Allowing ⅛″ clearance (minimum), bolt top track in place, Illus. 79, so door slides freely.

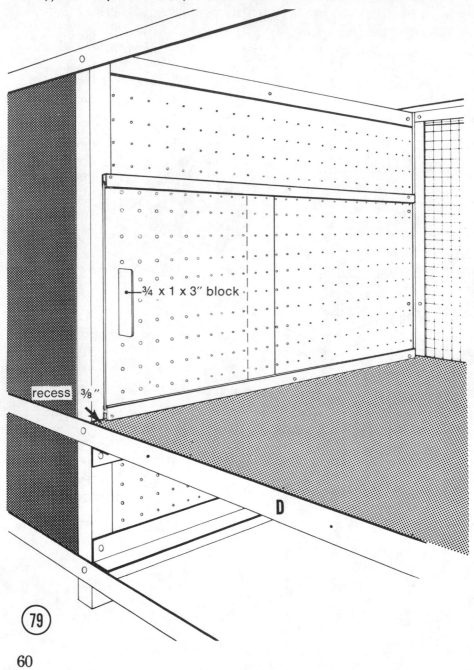

¾ x 1 x 3″ block

recess ⅜″

D

79

The sleeping compartment entry door can be cut from ⅛"
pegboard to size opening requires, or you can use ⅛ x ¾"
bar stock and wire mesh. Those who plan on building a quantity of catpartments should make a 1 x 2 jig, Illus. 80. This will
hold ⅛ x ¾" bar stock, Illus. 81, in place while drilling holes.
Measure opening for door. Build jig to overall size of opening
less ¼" in overall width and height. This allows ⅛" clearance
for door.

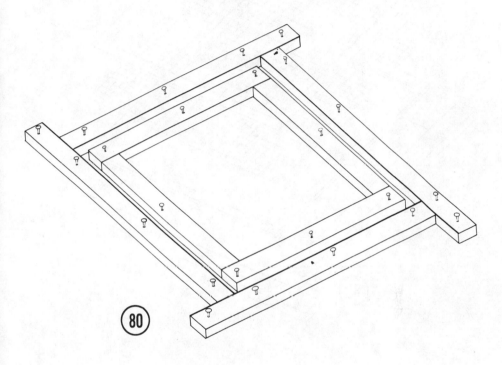

(80)

Drill through both pieces
of aluminum at dash lines

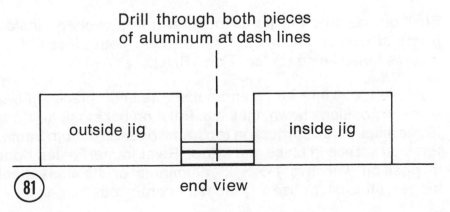

outside jig   inside jig

(81)   end view

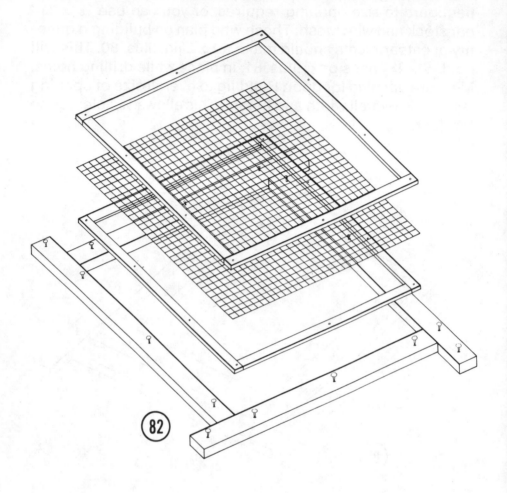

(82)

Position bar stock in jig so outside frame overlaps inside frame at corners, Illus. 82. Drill through both pieces. This insures holes lining up for "Pop" Rivets.

Remove 1 x 2″ interior jig and substitute short pieces of bar stock in position shown, Illus. 83. Position bar stock for door frame, Illus. 82, so corners on top frame overlap bottom frame. Position screen in place and "Pop" Rivet frame. Fasten door in position with two 1½ x 2″ aluminum or stainless steel hinges, Illus. 84, or use 2″ pieces of continuous hinge.

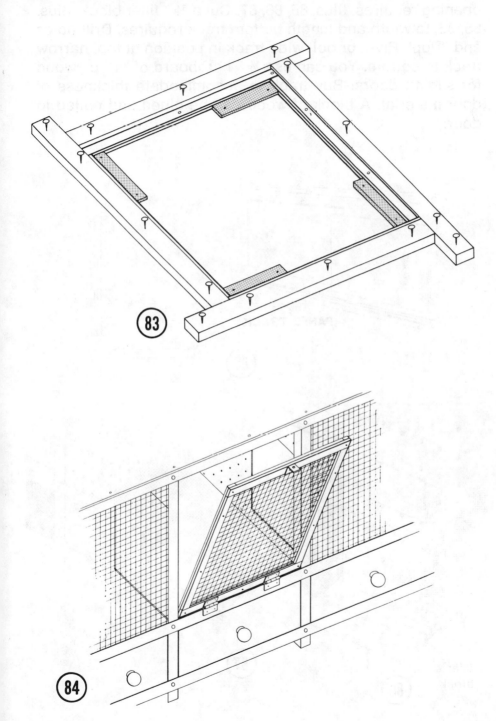

83

84

63

Cut two lengths of sliding door track for feeding door to size opening requires, Illus. 85, 86, 87. Cut a ⅝" filler block, Illus. 85, 86, to width and length bottom track requires. Drill holes and "Pop" Rivet or bolt wide track in position at top, narrow track to bottom. You can use ⅛" hardboard of ¼" plywood for sliding doors. Buy track to accommodate thickness of door material. A block of wood can be glued and nailed to door.

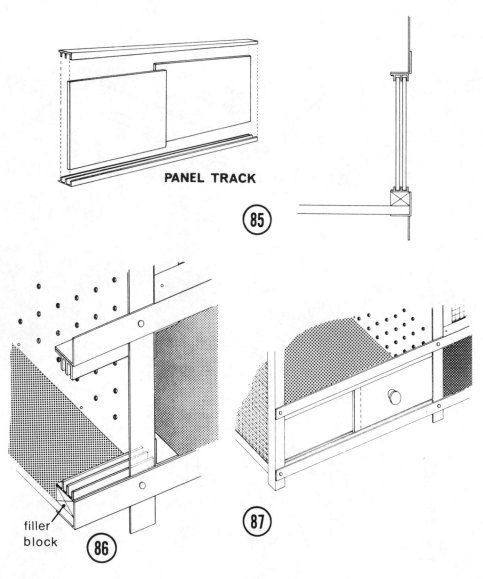

PANEL TRACK

85

filler block

86

87

A litter drawer, Illus. 88, can be assembled to size shown, or to size opening requires. Use ⅜" plywood. If drawer opening measures 14", cut two A — 4⅜ x 12⅞"; two B — 4⅜ x 23¼" one C — 13⅝ x 23¼"; one D — 4¾ x 13⅝". Glue and nail B to A, C to AB with 4 penny finishing nails. Glue and screw A to D. Drill and fasten a drawer pull in position. If you glue and nail ¾" quarter round in position shown, Illus. 89, then line the box with polyethylene before filling with kitty litter, it helps keep the drawer odor free.

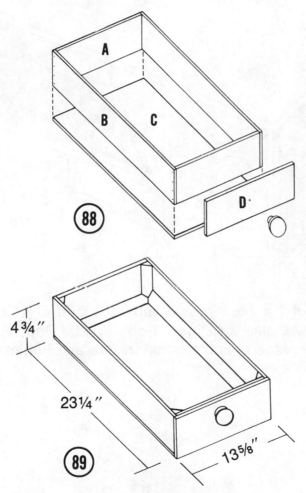

Build the same type of drawer to size opening requires for grooming tools. The drawer doesn't require the quarter round fillers.

"Pop" Rivet ⅛" perforated hardboard, aluminum, or plywood to top, Illus. 90. If aluminum is used, fasten in position with ⅛ x ¾" bar stock.

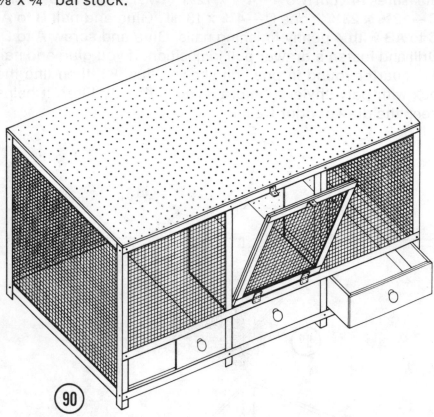

(90)

Cut pieces of 1 x 1 x 1" angle, Illus. 91. Drill a ¼" hole in position shown, also a ³⁄₁₆" for "Pop" Rivet. "Pop" Rivet in position over piece of angle on door. Use an aluminum bolt as a lock.

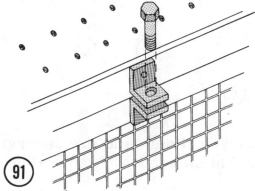

(91)

HOW TO BUILD A DUCK INN

Baby ducks fascinate every child. Learning to raise ducks provides an excellent experience in animal husbandry. It also offers income producing potential. Directions explain how to build a duck inn complete with a plastic swimming pool and sand beach. Since ducklings need supervision during their early swim, a partition separates the pool from the beach. Pet stores sell treated sand to hold down odors. Make certain the sand doesn't contain chemicals harmful to baby ducks.

Tempered hardboard, sheathing or exterior grade plywood can be used where indicated. Prime and paint all parts after cutting to size required.

To build a duck inn measuring 16 x 36 x 18″ high, you will need the following:

LIST OF MATERIALS
1 — ½ x 4 x 8′ plywood panel A, B, C, D, E
1 — plastic pan — approximately 11 x 13 x 5½″ deep
¼″ wire mesh — 16 x 36″
2 — ¼ x 1½″ aluminum bolts and washers

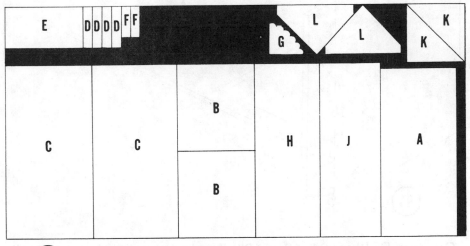

(92)

The cutting chart, Illus. 92, shows how to cut parts from one

67

panel. Cut A — 16 x 35", Illus. 93. Cut an opening in A, in position indicated, for plastic or rubber pan. Lipped edge holds pan in position. Cut opening to size lip requires. Test pan in position then remove pan until project is completely assembled and painted.

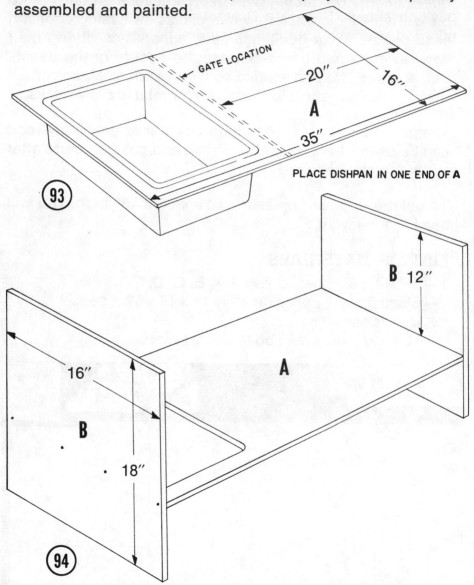

PLACE DISHPAN IN ONE END OF A

Cut two B, Illus. 94, 16 x 18". Apply waterproof glue to all parts before assembling. Nail B to A in position indicated with 6 penny finishing nails.

Cut two C, Illus. 95, 18 x 36″. Apply glue and nail C to B and A. Space nails about 4″ apart.

Cut four 1 x 2 x 12″ D, Illus. 95. Apply glue and nail D to C in position shown. Separate D amount equal to thickness of plywood used for gate E. E should slide easily between D.

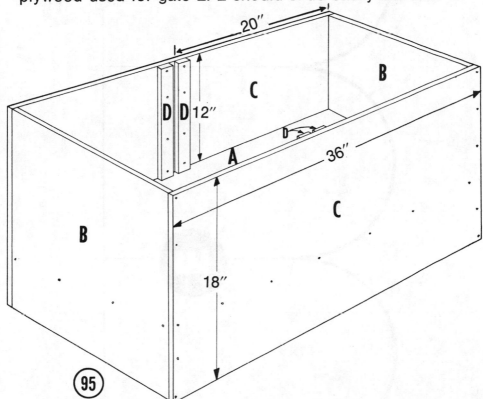

Cut one E, Illus. 96, 8½ x 16″. Trace pattern, Illus. 97, for top edge. Cut to shape shown with a coping or sabre saw.

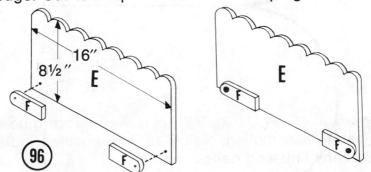

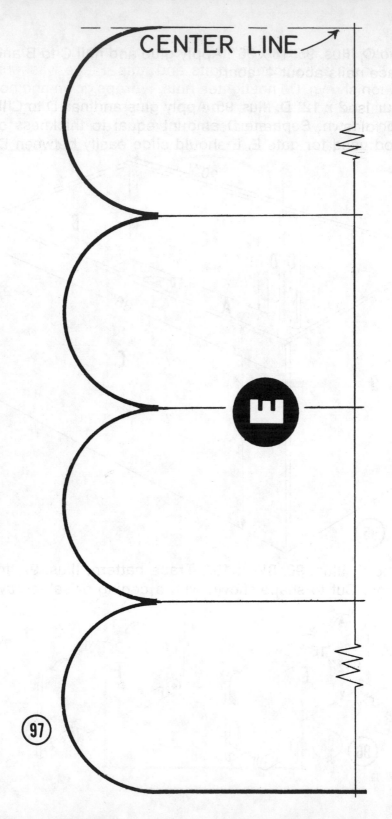

Cut two legs F, Illus. 98, to full size of pattern. Bolt F to E with ¼ x 1½″ aluminum bolts and nuts. Place washers in position shown. Do not tighten nuts. F drops down and holds E in raised position when the pool is open for action, Illus. 99. F folds down when gate is lowered, Illus. 100.

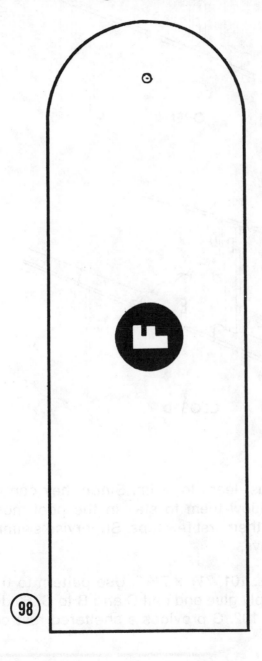

98

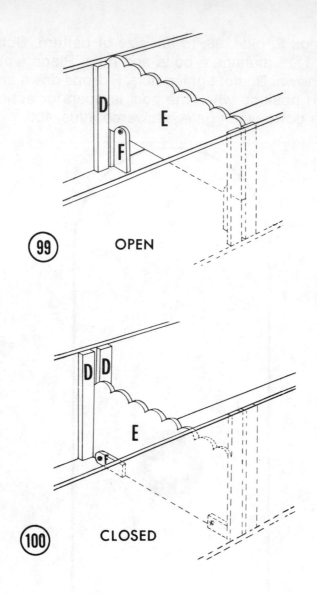

99 OPEN

100 CLOSED

Baby ducks must learn to swim. Since they can get water logged, don't allow them to stay in the pool more than 5 minutes during their first few dips. Supervise swimming during the early days.

Cut roof G, Illus. 101, 7¼ x 7¼". Use pattern to trace scalloped edge. Apply glue and nail C and B to G, 6" down from top edge, Illus. 102. G provides a sheltered rest corner.

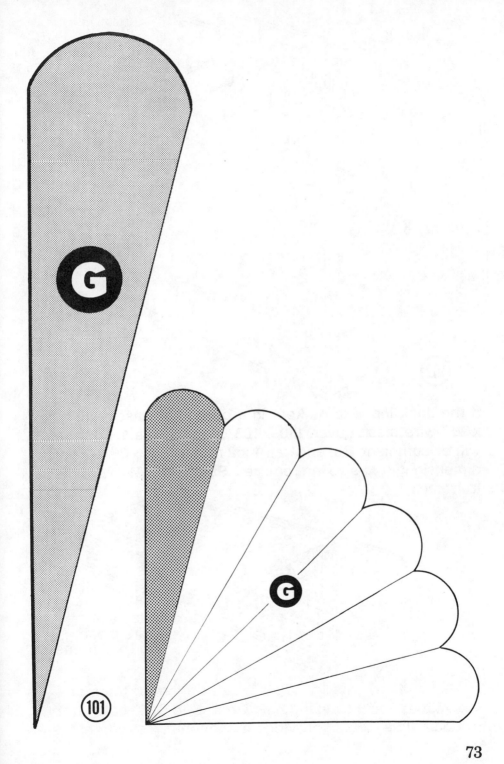

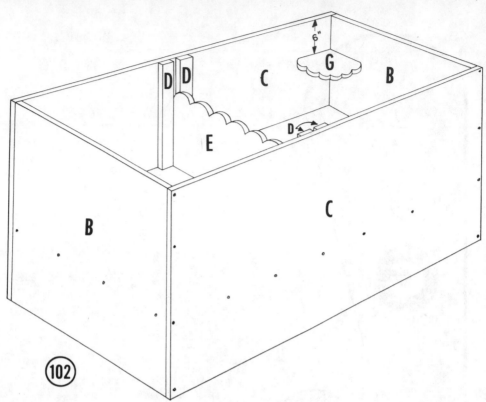

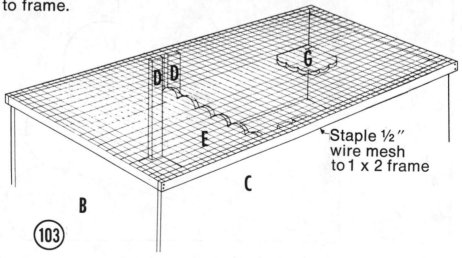

If the duck inn is to be kept in a garage or basement, a ½ x ½″ wire mesh cover, Illus. 103, stapled to a 1 x 2 frame, will be sufficient. Cut and nail 1 x 2 frame 16¼ x 36¼″ inside dimension, or to size inn requires. Staple ½ x ½″ wire mesh to frame.

Staple ½″ wire mesh to 1 x 2 frame

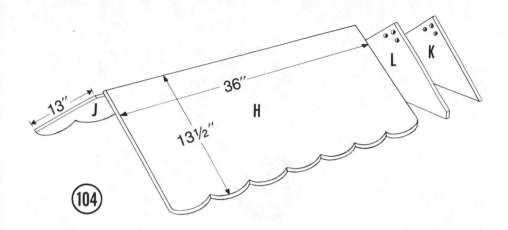

(104)

If the duck inn is to be placed outdoors, a removable roof H, J, Illus. 104, should be assembled. Cut one roof panel 13½ x 36″, the other 13 x 36″. Cut lower edge to shape shown, Illus. 105, 106.

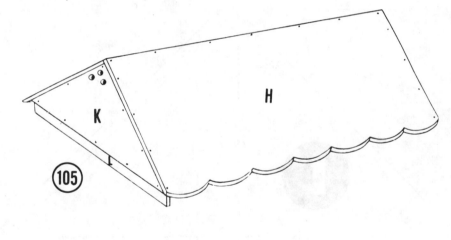

(105)

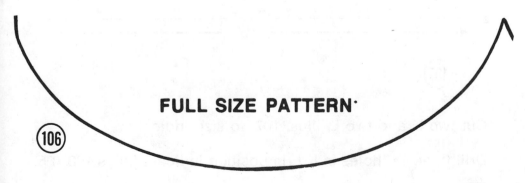

FULL SIZE PATTERN

(106)

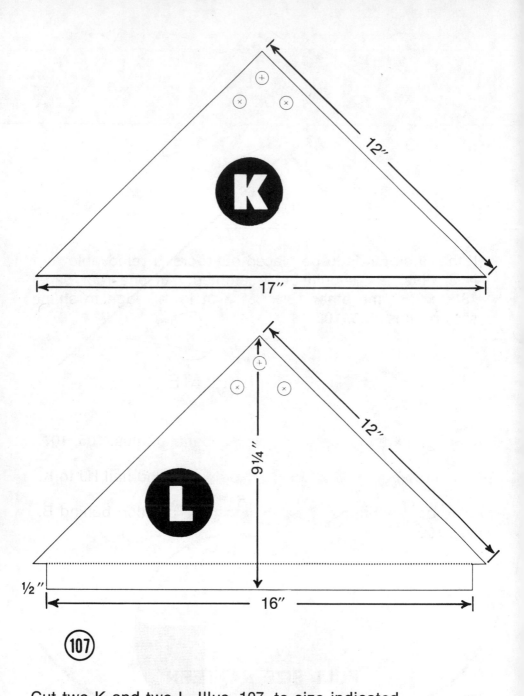

Cut two K and two L, Illus. 107, to size indicated.

Drill three ½″holes in K,L, in position indicated.Illus.108,105.

76

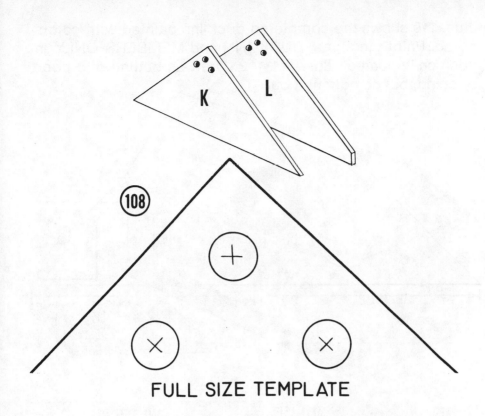

FULL SIZE TEMPLATE

Apply glue and nail roof panel H to panel J, Illus. 105, 107.

Glue and nail K to L, Illus. 107. Apply glue and nail HJ to K.

Plane or saw edge of L so it slides into position behind B, Illus. 109.

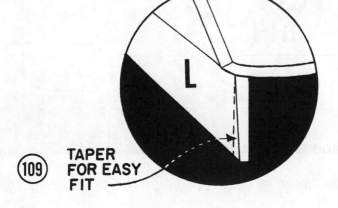

TAPER FOR EASY FIT

Illus. 110 shows the completed duck inn painted with colors noted. Paint the signs, DUCK INN and MEMBERS ONLY in position indicated, Illus. 111, 112. Draw an outline of a door opening, but do not cut it out.

PINK   BLUE   WHITE

110

DUCK
INN

3"
3"
6 3/4"
10"
6"
5"

111

SWIMMING
HOURS
9-11 A.M.   1-4 P.M.

(112)

Draw wave pattern, Illus. 113. This can be drawn so top of wave is about 6¾″ up from bottom of C and B. Paint the waves BLUE, with a darker blue line to outline the top of the wave.

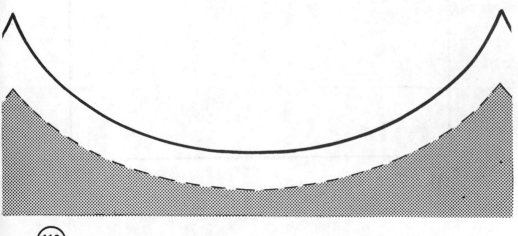

(113)

Illus. 114 shows another sign that can be painted on partition E, Illus. 115. Do not cut an opening in E.

DUCK INN
CLUB
MEMBERS ONLY

(114)

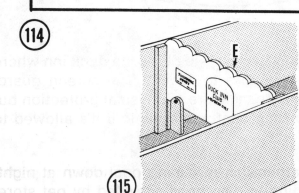

(115)

If the duck inn is to be used later as a duck house, cut door opening in C, 6″ wide by 10″ high as indicated, Illus. 111. If cut out is hinged at bottom, Illus. 116, it provides a ramp.

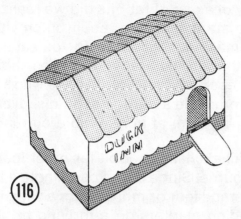

Since the edge of a plastic swimming pool may get slippery and make it difficult for baby ducks to get out of the pool, cut a ½ x 3 x 6″ swimming float, Illus. 117, and hook it over edge with two pices of coat hanger wire.

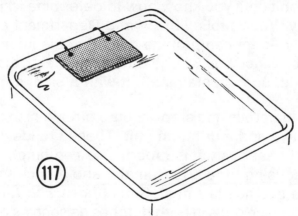

If you have a cat or dog, be sure to place the duck inn where they can't "scare the ducks to death." The screen guard, Illus. 103, provides some measure of physical protection but an inquisitive cat or dog can create panic if it's allowed to paw at the mesh.

Always keep the gate to the swimming pool down at night. Feed ducks according to directions provided by pet store.

RABBIT HUTCH

Everyone who shops a supermarket on a lean budget knows the problem of stretching a buck. Not until we noted the productive capacity of a pair of rabbits did we realize how much a buck could be stretched. The rabbit hutch illustrated is a food producing machine that can help you eat better, at less cost, than any other device. Rabbit provides choice cuts that many consider superior to chicken. Those who set up a "factory" alongside or inside a garage soon discover the poundage provides a new form of non-taxable currency.

Most markets will exchange rabbit for other food when they find a reliable source. Since a doe can kindle a litter in 29 to 32 days, and average four or more litters a year, the potential is sizeable. Leading markets do a thriving business selling rabbit the year round. They buy live rabbits.

The key to raising healthy rabbits rests in the selection of breeding stock, housing, feed and care. Don't buy or accept any gift rabbit until you know how to determine whether they are healthy. Your public library and Department of Agriculture County Agent can provide considerable information on this subject. Since you will be building a clean, disease free housing unit, don't contaminate it with a sick rabbit.

The list of materials and step-by-step directions explain how to build a two and four hutch unit. These are ideal for those who want to seriously raise food. The two hutch basic unit provides housing for a doe (female) and a buck (male). The hutch for a doe needs a nest. Since those who raise rabbits will want to place does in both hutches as soon as production starts, a separate cage, without a nest, should be constructed for the buck.

Rabbit is today a leading source of food in many emerging nations while consumption in the United States increases by millions of pounds each year. Encourage a youngster to raise rabbits as a business venture rather than as a pet. The time required to feed and clean the hutch could turn spare time into a steady income. The rabbits will help raise an adult equipped to face a major food problem of his generation. Hospitals and laboratories engaged in research are also potential volume buyers. Make phone calls to ascertain demand.

Raising rabbits provides retirees with a time consuming business opportunity. Not only does the poundage create extra income, but also a way to eat better at less cost. In some areas, the sale of skins can also produce income.

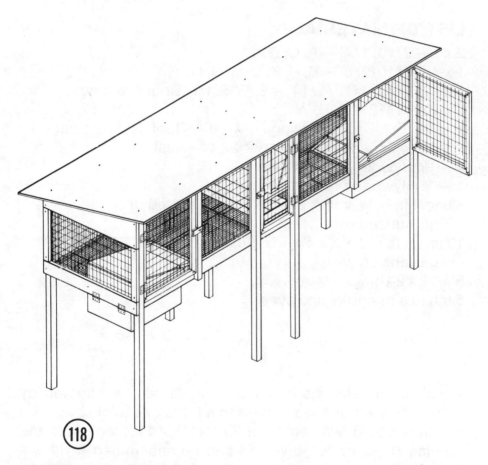

The hutch, Illus. 118, constructed according to directions provided, permits housing a doe and buck in separate compartments. Building as directions suggest, with a nest in each compartment, permits raising two litters at a time when the buck is housed in separate quarters. Always take the doe to the buck, Give them a few moments to make contact, then return the doe to her hutch. Never take the buck to the doe's hutch.

For complete details concerning the mating habits of rabbits, visit your Department of Agriculture County Agent, or request government bulletins on this subject.

LIST OF MATERIALS
2 x 2 — 2/10, 1/4′ — A, C, D
1 x 4 — 5/10, 2/8′ — B, H, K, L, M, N, O, T, Y
1 x 2 — 2/10, 1/12, 1/14′ — E, G, S, U — Door Framing
1 x 10 — 1/12 — P, R, W
1 — 3/8″ Ext. Grade Plywood — 4 x 8′ — Roof, Nest drawers, X
1 — 3/8″   ″   ″   ″   — 4 x 4′ — Nest
1 — 1/4 plywood — 2 x 2′ — V
1 — 3/4 plywood — 16 x 16″ — F
8 lineal ft. — 1/2 x 1/2 x 2′ wide plastic coated or
    galvanized wire
10 lineal ft. — 1 x 2 x 4′ wide plastic coated or
    galvanized wire
5 pr. 2 x 2″ hinges
5 latches or hooks and eyes

Considerable savings in material costs can be effected by those who own or have access to a table or radial saw. 2 x 4 can be sliced down center for 2 x 2 (1½ x 1½) legs A, C and framing D. 3/8 or ½″ plywood can be substituted for 1 x 4 and 1 x 2. Those who have any 1/8 or 3/16″ hardboard can substitute same for roof and floor of nest. The cutting charts show how to cut 3 x 8′ roof, nest, and parts for drawers from 3/8″ plywood.

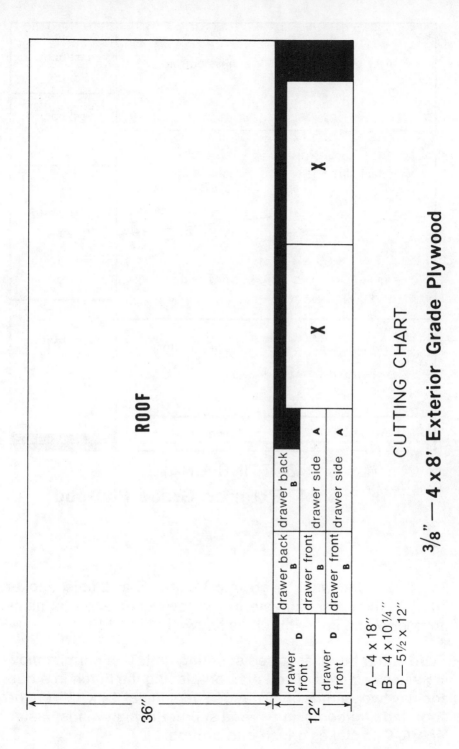

ROOF

36"

12"

drawer back **B** | drawer back **B**

drawer front **B** | drawer side **A**

drawer front **B** | drawer side **A**

drawer front **D**

drawer front **D**

X

X

A — 4 x 18"
B — 4 x 10¼"
D — 5½ x 12"

CUTTING CHART

3/8" — 4 x 8' Exterior Grade Plywood

85

nest bottom 12 x 18"	nest bottom	nest back 8 x 12"
		nest back
nest side 11½ x 18" nest side	nest side nest side	nest roof 12 x 15"
drawer bottom c 11 x 18"	drawer bottom c	nest roof
drawer side A	drawer side A	

CUTTING CHART
$3/8$" — 4 x 4' Exterior Grade Plywood

For those who want to go into business, a double decker hutch with recessed nests in the lower tier, and box nests on floor of the upper hutch, is shown in Illus. 119.

Build either hutch as a free standing unit. This permits moving when required. If you plan on placing the hutch in a garage, lay two lengths of 26 gauge sheet metal, 24 x 42", on the floor. If out of doors, in an area subject to high winds, fasten legs A, C to stakes driven into ground.

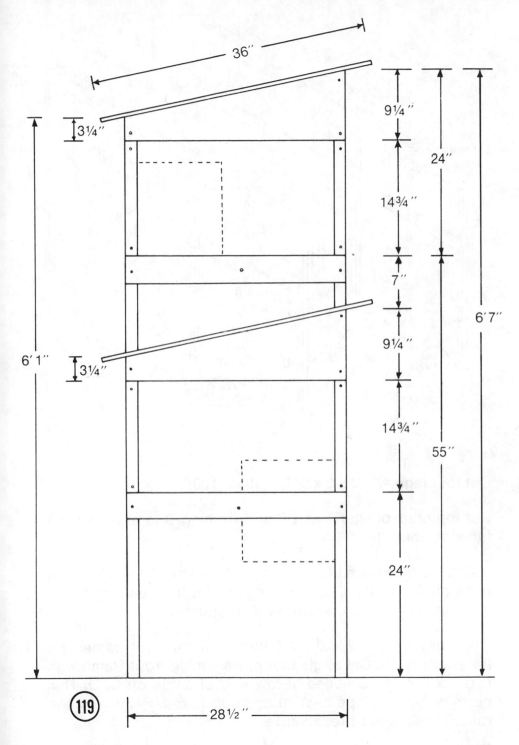

36″

3¼″

9¼″

24″

14¾″

6′7″

7″

9¼″

3¼″

14¾″

55″

6′1″

24″

119

28½″

87

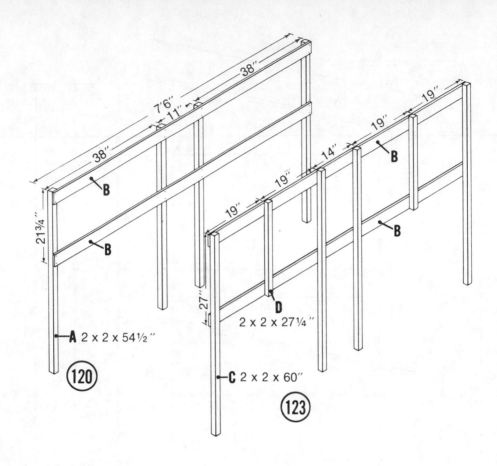

Cut four legs A — 2 x 2 x 54½″, Illus. 120.

Cut top ends of legs A and C and framing D to angle shown full size, Illus. 121.

Using two 8 penny nails at each joint, nail two 1 x 4 x 7′6″ B in position shown, Illus. 122. Top edge of B is flush with high side of angle on A. Check A and B with a square.

Cut four legs C — 2 x 2 x 60″, Illus. 123, for front frame; two 2 x 2 x 27¼″ D. Cut angle at top. Assemble front frame with two 1 x 4 x 7′6″ B nailed to low end of angle on C, D. This permits roof to slope back at angle required. Paint legs and rails B with wood preservative.

88

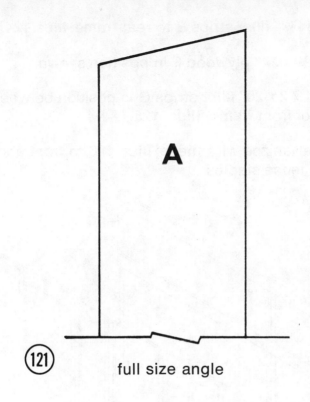

full size angle

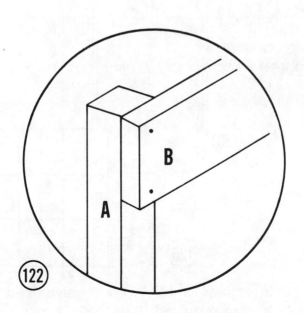

Nail 1 x 2 x 14¾" filler strips E to rear frame, Illus. 124.

Nail ¾ x 14¾ x 14" plywood F in position shown.

Nail four — 1 x 2 x 20" filler strips G in position between B on inside face of front frame, Illus. 125.

Nail 1 x 2 galvanized wire mesh, Illus. 126, to front and back frames with fence staples.

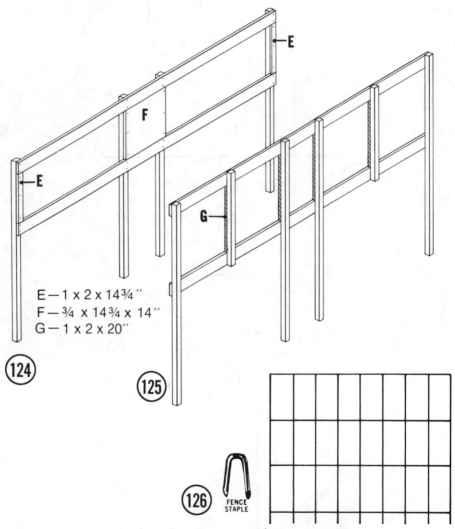

E — 1 x 2 x 14¾"
F — ¾ x 14¾ x 14"
G — 1 x 2 x 20"

124

125

126 FENCE STAPLE

If you buy 10 lineal feet of 48" — 1 x 2 galvanized, you can cut all panels to size required, Illus. 127.

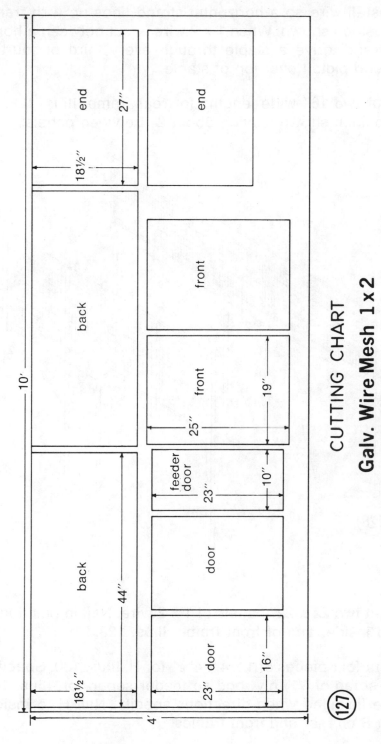

CUTTING CHART
Galv. Wire Mesh 1 x 2

127

91

Install wire so a horizontal strand lines up with framing in position shown. When 1 x 2 wire is cut between a horizontal strand, drive a staple through every third or fourth wire. Bend pigtail over top of staple.

Cut two 16″ wide lengths for rear frame, Illus. 128. Nail in position shown leaving about 2″ between panels.

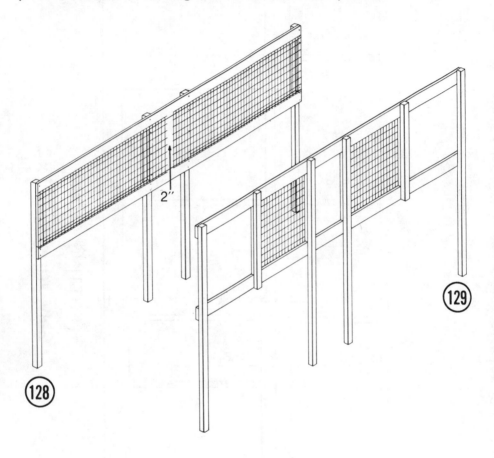

Cut two 22 x 22″ panels of 1 x 2 wire. Nail in position shown to inside face of front frame, Illus. 129.

Cut four pieces of 1 x 4 x 4⅝″ for H, Illus. 130. Space H with a scrap of ¼″ plywood so feeder separator, Illus. 142, can be installed when directions specify. Nail H to inside face of B on rear and front frames.

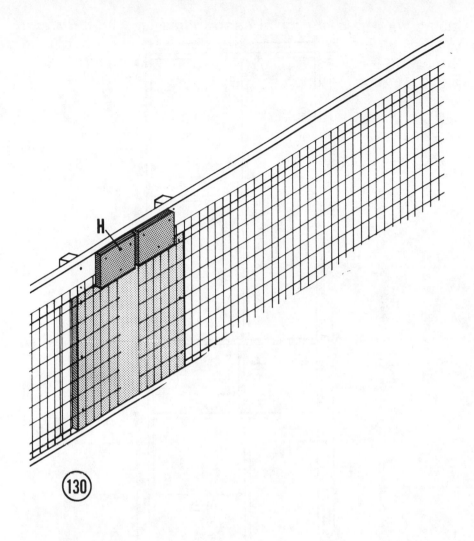

(130)

Assemble floor framing, Illus. 131. Cut four 1 x4 x 22½″ K; two 1 x 4 x 7′6″ L; two 1 x 4 x 38¾″ M; one 1 x 4 x 9½″ N; two 1 x 4 x 12¼″ O. Apply glue and nail L to K; K to M; K to N; LM to O with 6 penny finishing nails.

Check lengths of diagonals, Illus. 132. When diagonals are equal length frame is considered square. Hold square with 1 x 2 cross braces. Allow glue to set before proceeding.

Place rear frame on a flat surface and nail through L into BA with 4 penny nails.

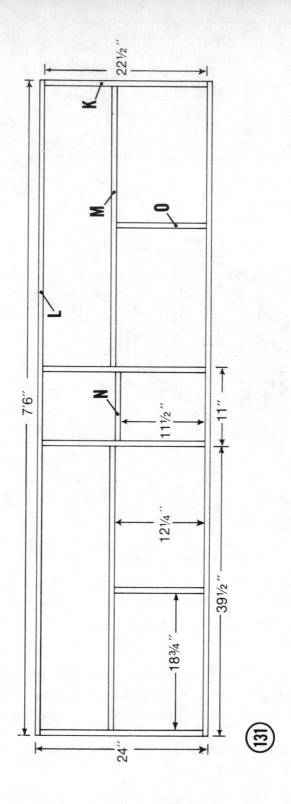

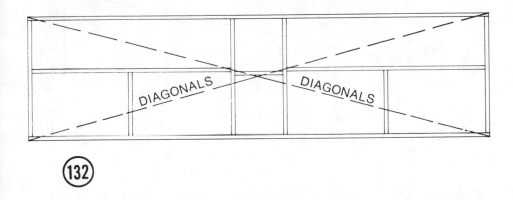

DIAGONALS   DIAGONALS

(132)

Place front frame on a flat surface and nail through L into BC, then through L into BA. Check assembled frame with a square, Illus. 133. Hold square with 1x2 temporary bracing.

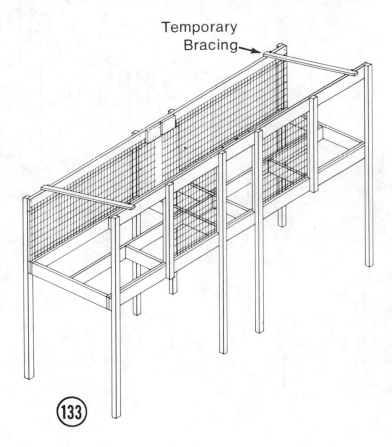

Temporary
Bracing

(133)

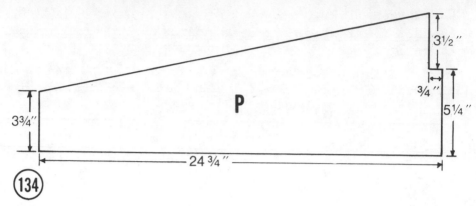

Cut two ¾″ plywood P to size and shape shown, Illus. 134.

Nail in position indicated, Illus. 135, to ends of H and side of G.

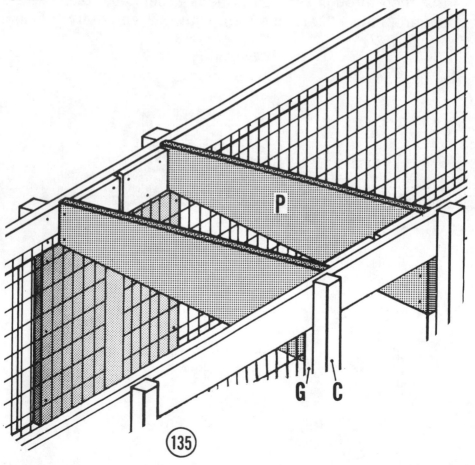

Cut and staple ½ x ½ x 24″ x 7′6″ wire mesh to K, L, M, N, O, Illus. 136. Keep smooth side of mesh up. If you plan on installing recessed nests, Illus. 155, cut openings in wire before stapling in place. To provide extra floor area when a litter starts roaming, cut a piece of wire to overall size of opening plus 1½″ in width and length. Staple wire to two 1 x 1 x 14″ strips, Illus. 136A. When you remove the nest, this panel covers opening.

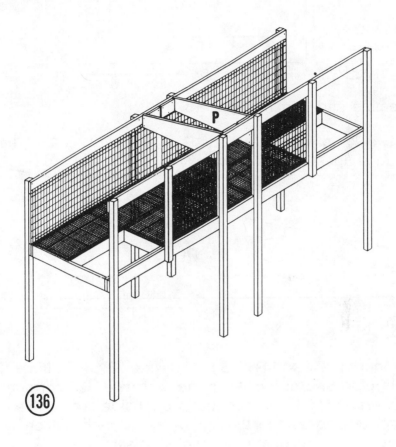

 136

136 a

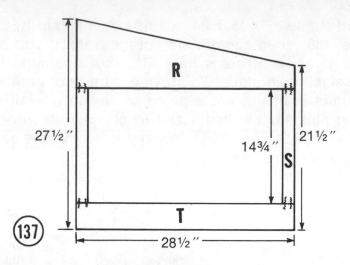

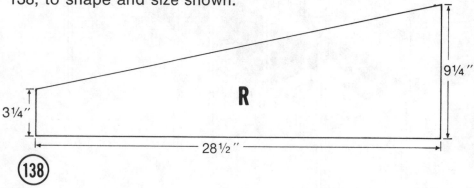

Assemble end framing, Illus. 137.

Cut two ¾" plywood top ends R — 3¼ x 28½ x 9¼", Illus. 138, to shape and size shown.

Cut four 1 x 2 x 14¾" S ; 1 x 4 x 28½" T, Illus. 137. Apply glue and assemble frame with two ⅜" corrugated fasteners about ⅜" in from edge on inside face. Drive one ⅜" corrugated fastener through center of each joint on other face. Check with square. Allow glue to set.

Apply 1 x 2 wire mesh to inside face, Illus. 139. Cut wire to size required.

Drill holes through R, S, T. Recheck framing with square and fasten assembled end, Illus. 140, in position with ten 1½" No. 8 flathead wood screws.

98

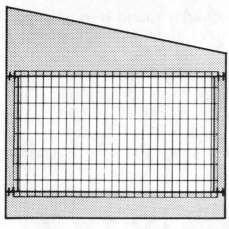

Corrugated
Fastener

(139)

(140)

Nail a 12″ length of ¾″ quarter round U in position shown using 3 penny finishing nails, Illus. 141. Butt end of quarter round against H.

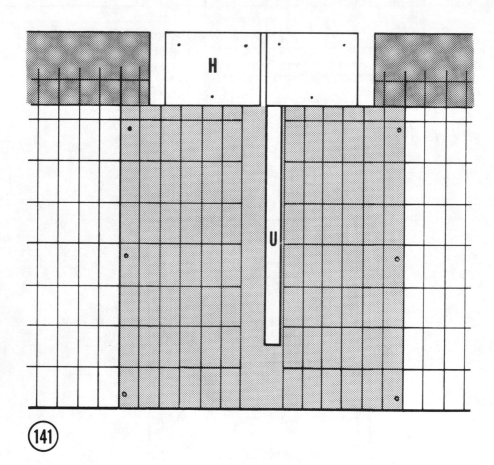

Cut plywood separator V, Illus. 142, to size shown. Insert V between H. Keep top edge level with P. Toenail in position with 3 penny finishing nails through H and U. Nail other U in position, Illus. 143.

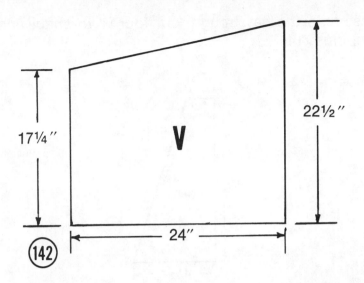

V

17¼″   22½″

24″

(142)

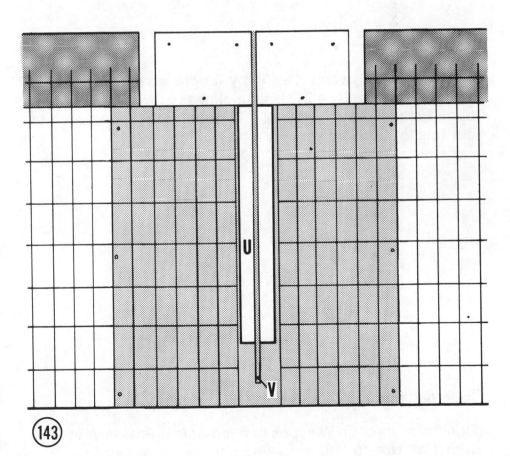

U

V

(143)

To assemble the hay trough, cut four W to shape and size shown, Illus. 144.

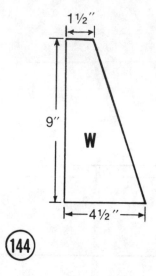

1½″

9″

W

|← 4½″ →|

(144)

Cut two ¼″ plywood X – 10″ by length needed, Illus. 145. Overall length will be 24″ less thickness of wire on front and back frame. The 10″ width of X is optional. You may want to cut this to 7 or 8″ if you use long cuttings.

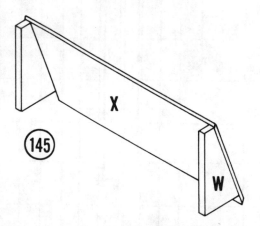

X

(145)

W

Glue and nail X to W with 3 penny finishing nails.

Drill holes through W in position indicated. Fasten W to F, G with 1½″ No. 10 flathead wood screws, Illus. 146.

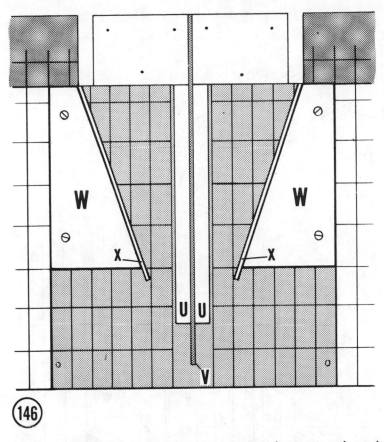

(146)

Or you can cut two pieces of sheet aluminum to size shown, Illus. 147, 148. Bend along A 90°. Bend along B 180°. Nail in position shown for W.

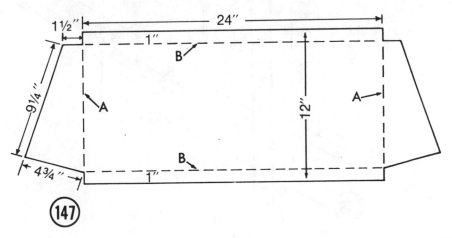

(147)

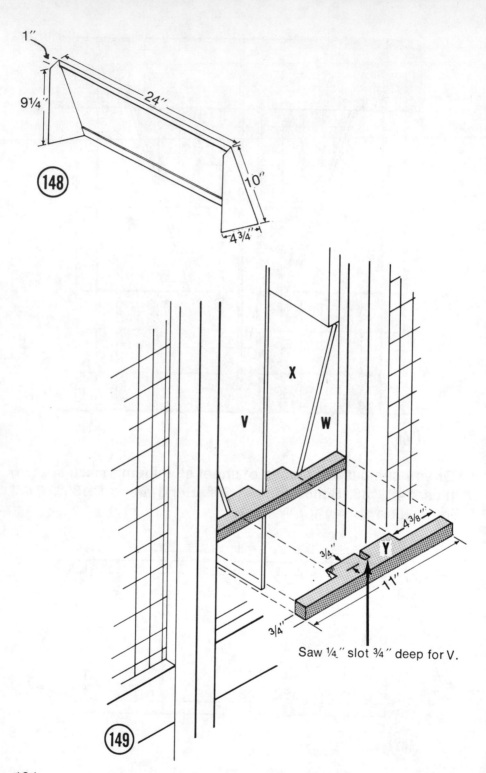

1″

9¼″

24″

10″

4¾″

(148)

X

V

W

4³/₈″

¾″

Y

V

11″

¾″

Saw ¼″ slot ¾″ deep for V.

(149)

104

Cut Y to overall size shown, Illus. 149. Y acts as a stiffener for V.

Buy a plastic, rubber or metal tray 2″ deep, 6 to 8″ wide by 12 to 20″. Notch top back edge of tray at center so it slides easily under V, Illus. 150. Use this tray for pellets. Fill rack with hay. An aluminum foil tray or one shaped from sheet aluminum can also be used.

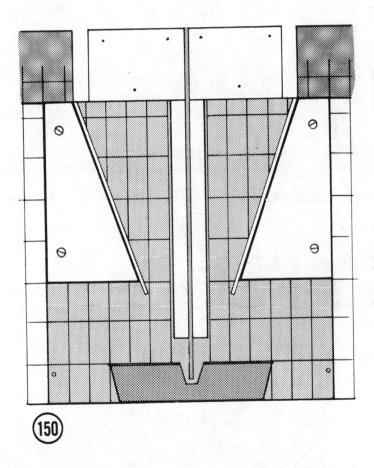

(150)

Build feeder door, Illus. 151. Miter cut two 1 x 2 x 10¾″; two 1 x 2 x 23″. Apply glue and fasten corners with two ⅜″ corrugated fasteners on inside face. Check with square. Allow glue to set. Cut 1 x 2 wire 10 x 22″ and staple in position to inside face of door.

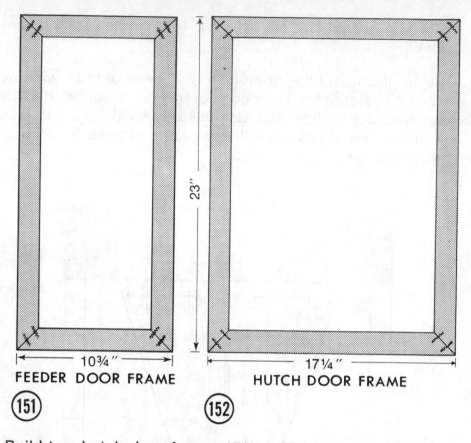

23"

FEEDER DOOR FRAME

(151)

HUTCH DOOR FRAME

(152)

Build two hutch door frames 17¼ x 23″, Illus.152. Miter cut four 1 x 2 x 17¼″; four 1 x 2 x 23″. Assemble following procedure outlined. Staple 1 x 2 wire to inside face of frame.

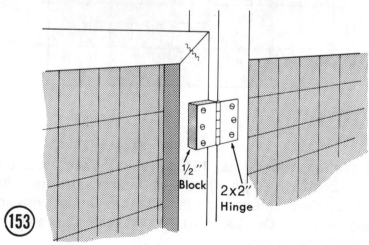

½″ Block

2x2″ Hinge

(153)

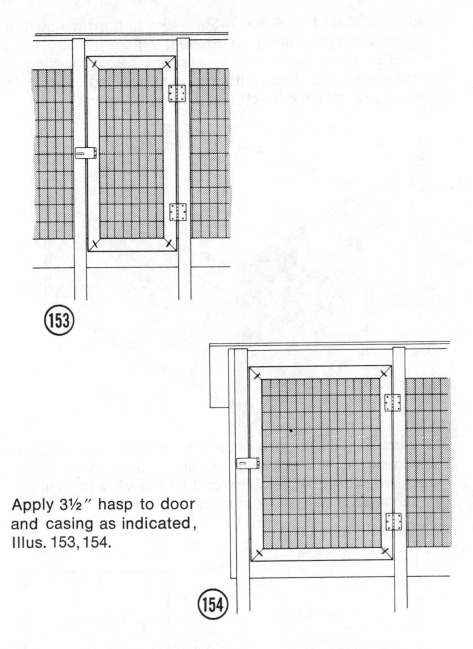

(153)

Apply 3½″ hasp to door
and casing as indicated,
Illus. 153, 154.

(154)

To fasten hinges flush with legs, cut ½″ plywood blocks to
size of hinge. Nail to door, Illus. 153. Drill holes through block
and fasten 2 x 2″ fast pin hinges, 3½″ down from top of door,
3½″ up from bottom, with 1¼″ No. 8 flathead wood screws
into door framing. Use 1″ No. 8 screws in leg, Illus. 154.

Build nest, Illus. 155. Since rabbits like to burrow down, if you build a nest that hangs in opening in floor framing, Illus. 133, the doe will line it with fur and hay before kindling. A completely enclosed box with a hole in one end, placed on floor in corner of each hutch could be substituted.

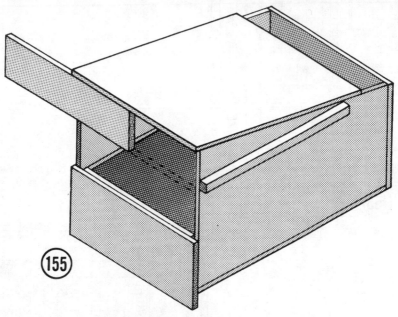

(155)

Cut parts for nest to size shown, Illus. 156. Glue and nail back to sides; ⅛″ tempered pegboard*floor to sides; ⅛″ hardboard roof to sides. Glue and nail ¾ x ¾ x 14″ hangers to each side of box, 8″ from bottom.

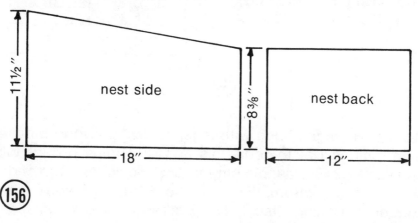

11½″

nest side

8⅜″

nest back

18″

12″

(156)

* ⅛ or ³⁄₁₆″ hardboard can also be used

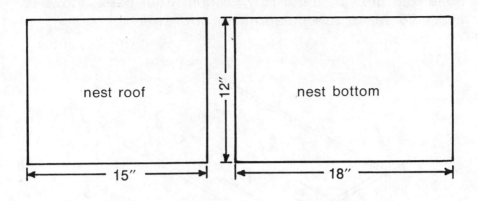

nest roof

nest bottom

12″

15″

18″

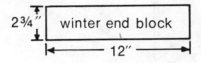

2¾″

winter end block

12″

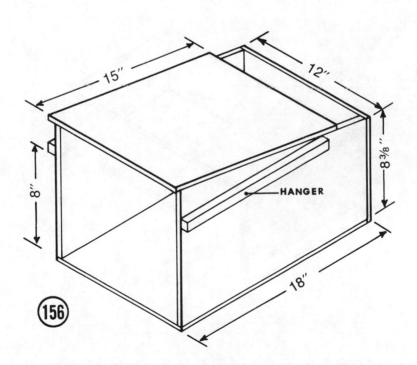

15″

12″

8⅜″

8″

HANGER

18″

(156)

Assemble drawer, Illus. 157, for nest from parts shown in Illus. 158. Make saw cuts in floor of drawer.

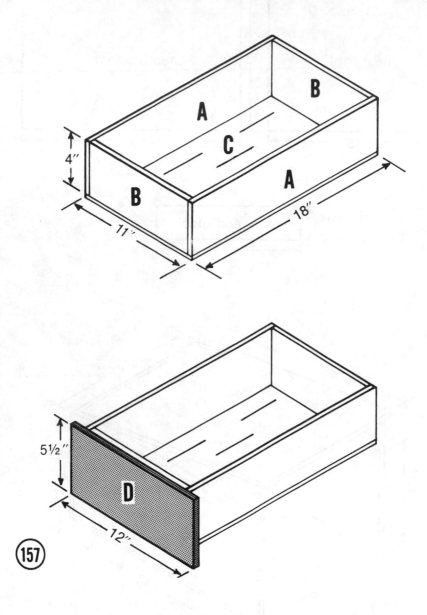

Glue and nail A to B; C to AB; D to B. Keep D flush with top edge of AB. Lipped bottom edge provides a drawer pull.

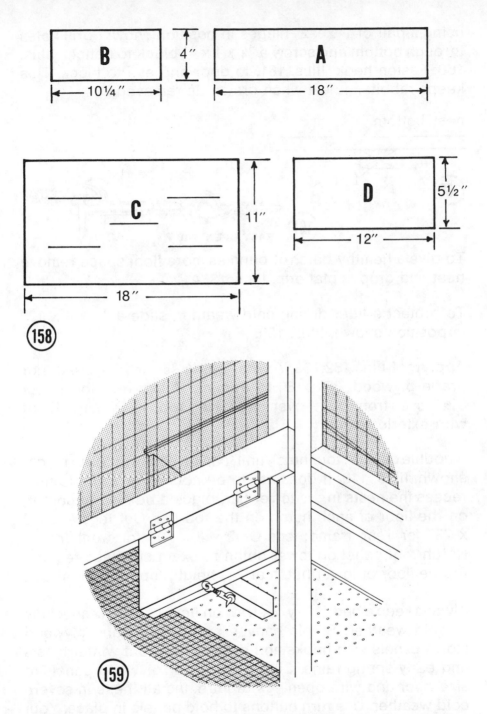

Install nest drawer door, Illus. 159. Since you will want to remove nest drawer to clean, hinge a ¾ x 5½ x 12″ door using a pair of 1½ x 2″ hinges in position shown. Drill holes through bottom and screw a ¾ x 1 x 4″ block to bottom, Illus. 160. Fasten hook, Illus. 161, to door and eye to block. This keeps rabbits in nest when drawer is removed.

nest bottom

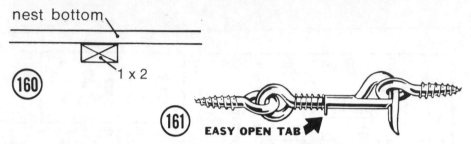

1 x 2

(160)

(161) EASY OPEN TAB

To give a healthy batch of bunnies more floor space, remove nest and drop in platform, Illus. 136A.

To protect a litter during cold weather, slide a ¾ x 4 x 12″ in position shown, Illus. 155.

Apply roof, Illus. 162, 163. You can nail ¼, ⅜″ or heavier exterior grade plywood, 36″ x 8′, to framing. Allow roof to project 3½″ over front, 2¼″ over ends. Nail roof to framing. Paint with exterior paint.

A double decker, four hutch unit, can be constructed to height shown, Illus. 119. If does are to be housed in all four units, recess the nests in the lower tier, place a box in the corner, on the floor of each hutch on the top tier. Cut legs A 2 x 2 x 73″ for rear frame; legs C 2 x 2 x 79″ for front frame. Notch roof panel on lower hutch to exact size legs require. Frame floor of lower hutch at 24″ height; upper floor at 55″.

Always keep a bed of hay or straw on floor of hutch especially in cold weather. Staple canvas curtains or hang plywood storm panels with hooks and eyes to keep out winter blasts and early spring rains. Cut ¼, ⅜ or ½″ plywood panels to size door and wire openings require. Install these in severe cold weather. Use turn buttons to hold panels in place. Your Department of Agriculture County Agent can give you much good advice concerning the care of small animals.

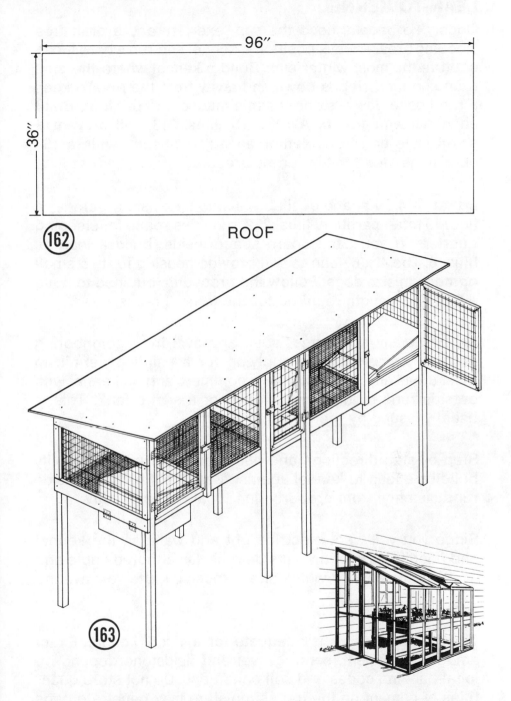

$\overset{\text{(162)}}{}$ ROOF

96″

36″

$\overset{\text{(163)}}{}$

Grow greens the year round in an easy to build walk-in or window greenhouse. Book #611 explains HOW.

LEAN-TO KENNEL

Dogs, like people, need the sun, exercise and a draft free sleeping area. Always position a kennel and run where it can capture the most winter sun. Build a kennel where the surrounding land slopes down and away from the run. To keep a run hosed down, slope it a minimum of ¼" per foot. Build each run with a curb. A 10" curb, Illus. 213, will prevent a small male dog from wetting an adjacent run, while a 16" curb is needed for the larger breeds.

If there's 4' of space available inside an existing garage, a floor to rafter partition, Illus. 222, provides space for sleeping quarters. If you can't spare space inside, build a lean-to, Illus. 6. The 4' x 6' lean-to will provide housing for two small or medium size dogs. Follow the procedure outlined to build a 6' x 8', or length required for the larger breeds.

As previously suggested, seek approval from neighboring property owners before applying for a building permit. In most areas an application for a commercial type kennel with outside runs requires installation of a septic tank. This is usually issued by the Board of Health.

Step-by-step directions and assembly illustrations simplify building a lean-to kennel against a garage. Position outside runs distance from property line local codes specify.

Since you will want electric light and water in the kennel and floodlights over the outside runs, lay armored cable and a plastic or copper water line in position after excavating foundation.

The list of materials is adequate for a 4' x 6' kennel. Exact amount of cement, sand, gravel and fieldstone depend on local building codes and soil conditions. Do not store quantities of cement on the job as moisture may penetrate bags and harden it. As a starter, order:

114

LIST OF MATERIALS

5 bags cement, 2 yds. sand, 3 yds. gravel or amount required
Five ⅜″ x 4 x 8′ Ext. Grade Plywood
2 x 4 — 6/14, 6/12′
2 x 3 — 1/8′
1 x 4 — 2/14, 3/12, 3/10′
1 x 2 — 1/14′
5/4 x 4 — 1/4′
9/32″ x 1 — (¾″) Lattice — 1/8′
Four ½ x 8″ Machine Bolts and eight Washers
1 box ⅝″ Corrugated Fasteners
Three 4″ Heavy Duty T Hinges
One 3⅓″ Hasp
2 lbs. 6d Common Nails
1 lb. 16d   ″   ″
5 lbs. 2″ Galvanized Big-Head Roofing Nails
1 lb. 8d Finishing Nails
¼ lb. 1¼″ Galvanized Big-Head Roofing Nails
One 6′6″ length of 9″ wide Aluminum Flashing
Finished Roofing to cover 30 sq. ft.
Exterior Paint
2 Pulleys,
4 Screw Eyes
2 Cleats

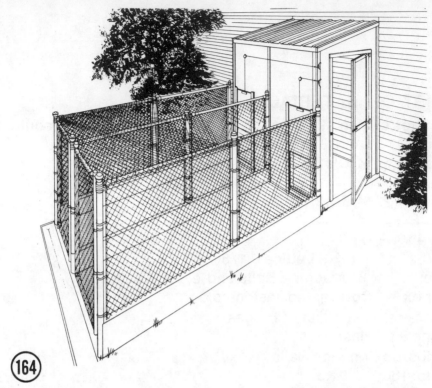

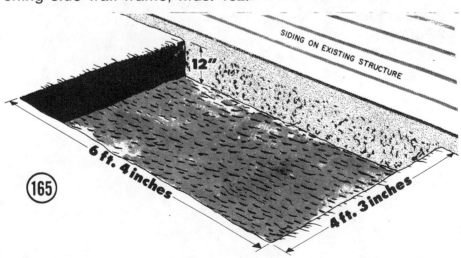

The construction of a lean-to kennel follows this general procedure. A two dog kennel for the smaller breeds can be built to size indicated, Illus. 164,165. This provides two 3′ wide runs. You can add as many more runs as desired by lengthening side wall frame, Illus. 182.

Excavate area approximately 12″ deep, 4′3″ wide x 6′3″ long or to size desired. In cold areas, building codes recommend excavating to a depth below frost level. Dig trenches, Illus. 166, to depth required.

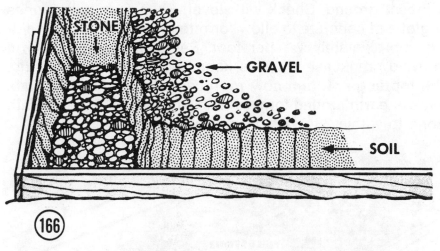

(166)

Build a 2 x 6 foundation form, Illus. 167. Keep inside dimensions to size indicated or to size desired. Hold form square with 1 x 4 temporary braces across corners. To make certain form is square, measure diagonals using a steel tape. Form is considered square when diagonals are equal length.

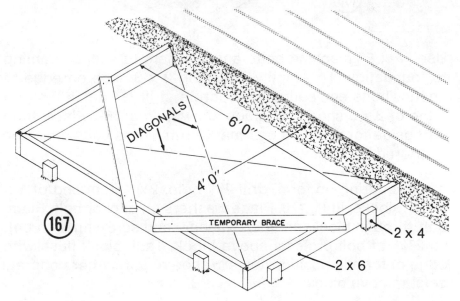

(167)

117

Place form on site selected. This will help you visualize size and its relation to your home and garage.

Place foundation form around excavated area, Illus. 168. Top edge should not be less than 4″ above highest point of adjacent ground. Check with level. Shim form with stones or globs of concrete to allow form to slope away from building approximately ½″ per foot. Paint inside face of form with old crankcase oil. This keeps concrete from sticking. The top edge of form now represents top of finished slab. Backfill earth around form to hold in position. Fill area with stone to within 2 to 2½″ from top of form.

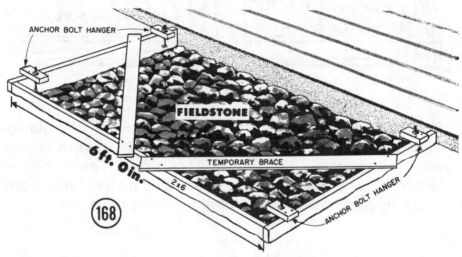

Use ⅜ x 8″ machine bolts and washers to anchor framing to foundation. To simplify installing 2 x 3 shoe on edge to anchor bolts embedded in concrete, drill ½″ holes through edge of 2 x 3 shoe in position shown, Illus. 169. Place shoe alongside form so you can mark form where bolts are to be anchored in concrete.

After squaring up form, drill ⅜″ hole, 2¼″ from end of 1 x 4 x 4″ blocks, Illus. 170. Place washers on anchor bolt. Place bolt through block, another washer, and screw nuts on bolt so 2¾″ of bolt projects above block. Tack block flush with edge of form in position holes in shoe require. After concrete sets, remove blocks.

118

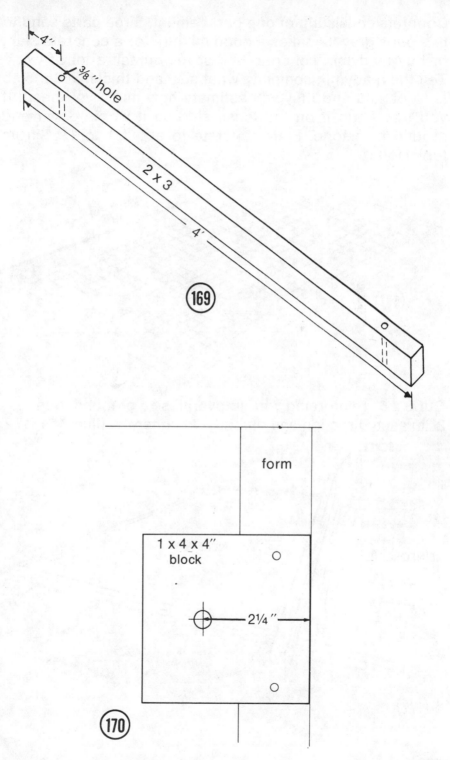

4"

3/8" hole

2 x 3

4'

169

form

1 x 4 x 4"
block

2¼"

170

119

Concrete consisting of one part cement, three parts sand to five parts gravel, makes a good mixture for a concrete slab, or buy readymix concrete and save yourself a lot of work. Tell the readymix company what size and thickness of slab is to be laid and they will estimate how much you need. If you mix, keep it on the loose side so it works down and around fieldstone. Pour concrete to about 1 to 1½" from top of form.

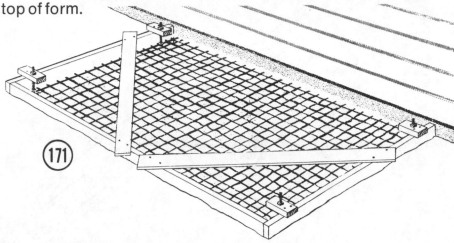

Cut 6 x 6" reinforcing wire to overall size of foundation less 2" in each direction and embed it in concrete, Illus. 171, 172.

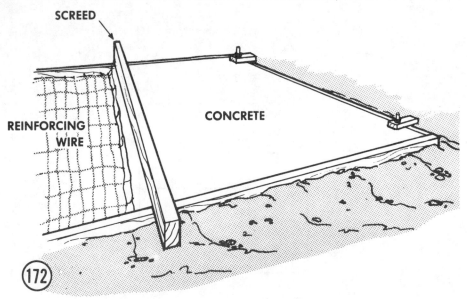

Finish pouring concrete to top edge of form. Work concrete back and forth with a 2 x 4 screed, Illus. 172. You can "float" (smooth) the concrete after it starts to set with a steel or wood float, Illus. 173, 174. Dip float in water as you smooth surface.

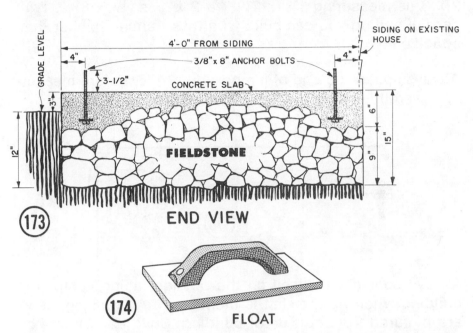

END VIEW

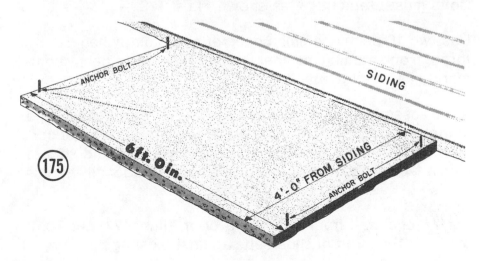

FLOAT

Allow slab to set three days before removing forms or doing any work on foundation. Spray slab once a day to help cure it properly. Backfill earth around slab, Illus. 175.

FRAMING

Due to the variance in lumber width and thickness cut all inner framing members to length needed to maintain overall dimensions indicated in assembly illustrations. We figured a 2 x 3 as measuring 1½ x 2½″; a 2 x 4 as 1½ x 3½″. With careful cutting you can build with less framing lumber than specified.

Always square up end of lumber, Illus. 176, before measuring overall length.

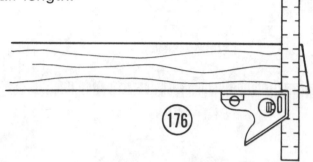

Always consider yourself on the outside facing completed building when right or left is mentioned. All framing views are pictured from outside of building. Build each frame on a flat level surface. Use 2 x 3 and 2 x 4 where specified. As illustrations indicate, the 2 x 3 shoe and studs Y and Z are installed flatwise. This requires using ⅜ x 8″ anchor bolts. Bolts must project 3½″ as shown, Illus. 173.

Use two 16 penny common nails at each joint when nailing through one framing member into another. Use 8 penny common nails when toenailing.

After assembling frame, check diagonals with a steel tape to make certain diagonals are equal length. Hit frame at corners with hammer if necessary to square up. Hold square with a 1 x 2 or 1 x 6 temporary brace nailed diagonally across studs.

For an end wall frame without a door, Illus. 177, cut 2 x 3 shoe 3′10½″. End of shoe butts against existing building.

122

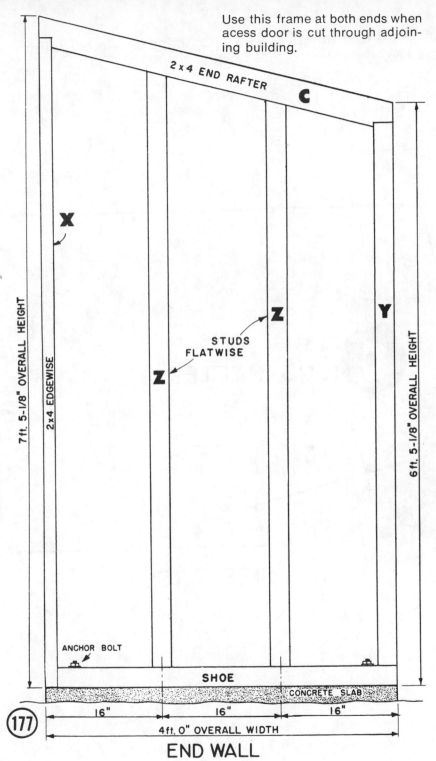

Use this frame at both ends when acess door is cut through adjoining building.

2 x 4 END RAFTER

C

X

Z

Z

STUDS
FLATWISE

Y

7 ft. 5-1/8" OVERALL HEIGHT

2 x 4 EDGEWISE

6 ft. 5-1/8" OVERALL HEIGHT

ANCHOR BOLT

SHOE

CONCRETE SLAB

(177)

16"   16"   16"

4 ft. 0" OVERALL WIDTH

END WALL

Cut 2 x 4 end rafters C 4'2¼₆" to shape shown on pattern, Illus. 178.

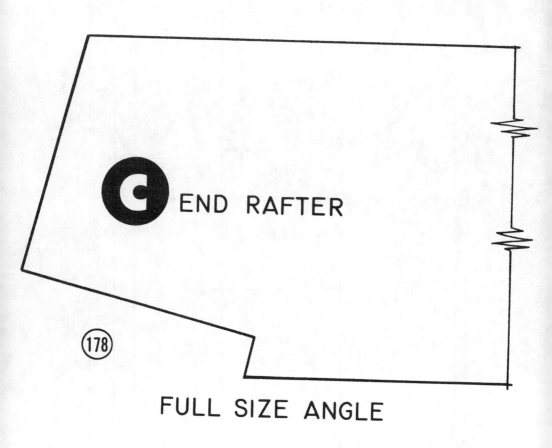

END RAFTER

(178)

FULL SIZE ANGLE

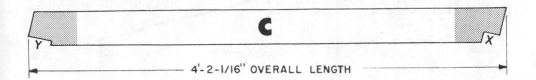

C

Y   X

4'- 2-1/16" OVERALL LENGTH

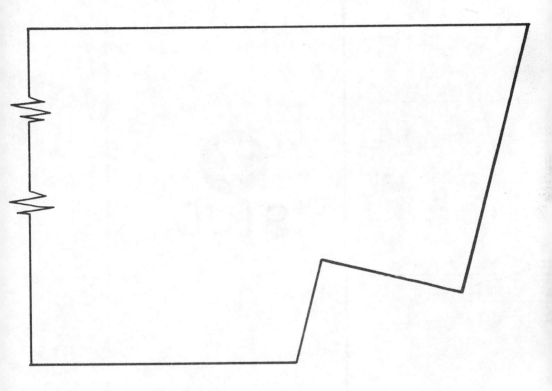

Cut 2 x 4 studs X 7'2⅛".

Cut 2 x 3 studs Y 5'11⅞".

Nail X, Y, C and shoe with 8 penny nails. Keep outside edge of X flush with outside face of C and shoe.

Cut 2 x 3 studs Z to length required to maintain overall dimensions noted, Illus. 177. The top end of studs Z are cut to angle shown, Illus. 179.

FULL SIZE
ANGLE

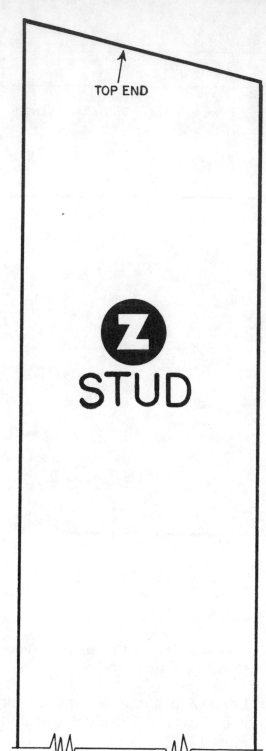

TOP END

Z
STUD

(179)

126

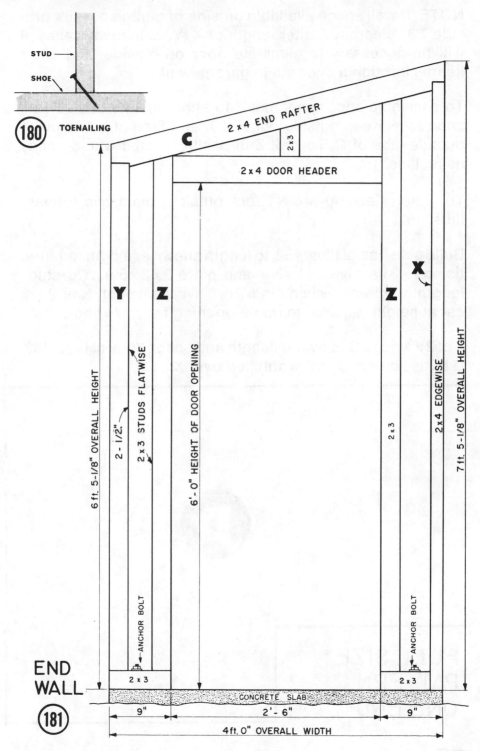

STUD →

SHOE

180 TOENAILING

2 x 4 END RAFTER

C

2 x 3

2 x 4 DOOR HEADER

Y

Z

Z

X

2 - 1/2"

2 x 3 STUDS FLATWISE

6 ft. 5-1/8" OVERALL HEIGHT

6'- 0" HEIGHT OF DOOR OPENING

2 x 3

2 x 4 EDGEWISE

7 ft. 5-1/8" OVERALL HEIGHT

ANCHOR BOLT

ANCHOR BOLT

2 x 3

2 x 3

END WALL

181

CONCRETE SLAB

9"

2'- 6"

9"

4 ft. 0" OVERALL WIDTH

NOTE: If wall space available on side of garage doesn't provide 7'6" clearance, alter length of X, Y, Z. In many cases, it will be necessary to eliminate door on outside, and enter kennel through a door cut in garage wall.

To assemble end frame, nail X to shoe, toenail C to X. Nail shoe to Y. Keep outside edge of X and face of Y flush with outside face of C. Toenail Z in position noted with 6 penny nails, Illus. 180.

To enter sleeping areas from outside, build two frames, Illus. 181.

Build side frame, Illus. 182, to length shown or length required using 2 x 3 flatwise. Cut shoe and plate 2 x 3 x 5'9". Cut studs length required to maintain 6'2½" overall height. Nail 2 x 3 cat at height required to frame opening for entry door.

Cut 2 x 4 ridge D to overall length and shape shown, Illus. 183. D butts against C and is notched over X.

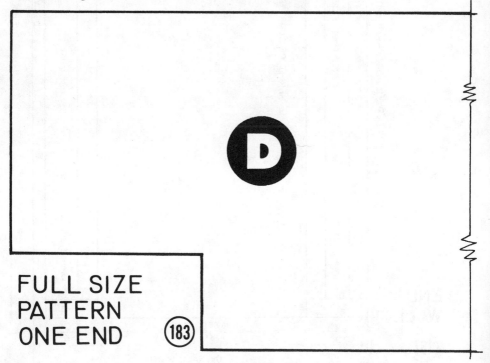

FULL SIZE PATTERN ONE END (183)

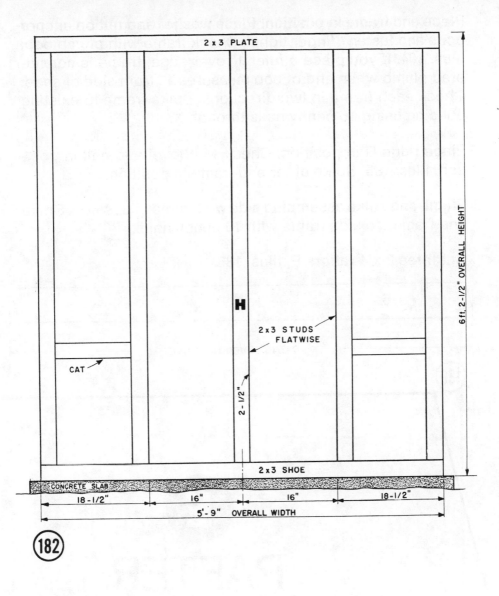

2 x 3 PLATE

6 ft. 2-1/2" OVERALL HEIGHT

H

2 x 3 STUDS
FLATWISE

2 - 1/2"

CAT

2 x 3 SHOE

CONCRETE SLAB

18-1/2"   16"   16"   18-1/2"

5'- 9" OVERALL WIDTH

(182)

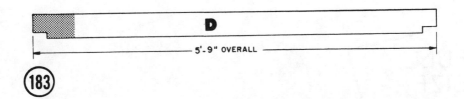

D

5'-9" OVERALL

(183)

129

Place end frame in position. Place washer and nut on anchor bolts and fasten "finger tight." Check frame with plumb bob, Illus. 184. If you place a ruler 1″ over edge, frame is considered plumb when end of bob measures 1″ from side of shoe. Check each frame in two directions. Spike frame to existing building using 16 penny nails through X.

Place ridge D in position. Check with level and nail in position, Illus. 185. Spike other end frame in position.

Plumb and spike assembled side wall frame in position. Spike end frames to side frame with 16 penny nails.

Cut three 2 x 4 rafters E, Illus. 186.

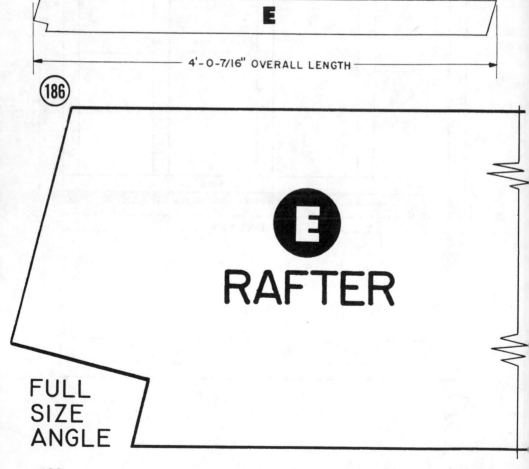

E

4'-0-7/16″ OVERALL LENGTH

186

E RAFTER

FULL SIZE ANGLE

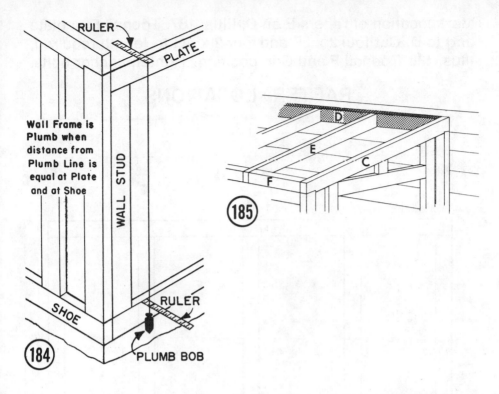

RULER

PLATE

Wall Frame is
Plumb when
distance from
Plumb Line is
equal at Plate
and at Shoe

WALL STUD

SHOE

RULER

184

PLUMB BOB

185

D

E

C

F

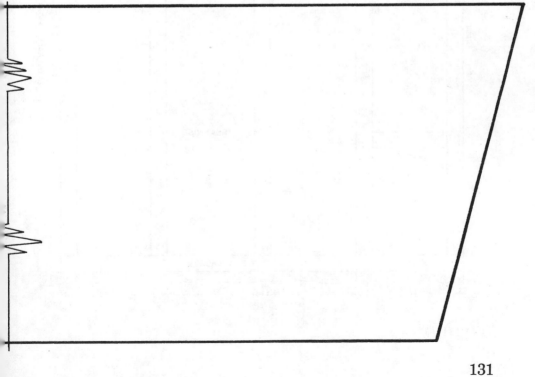

Mark location of rafters E on D, Illus. 187. Toenail E to plate and to D. Cut four 2 x 3F and four 2 x 4G to length required, Illus. 188. Toenail F and G in position. Tighten anchor bolts.

RAFTER LOCATIONS

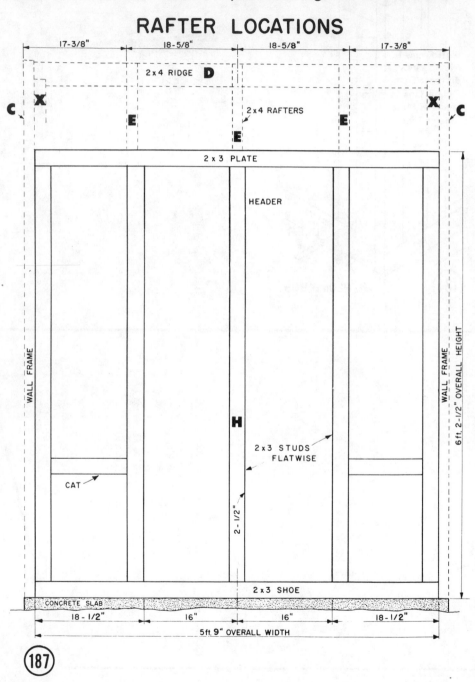

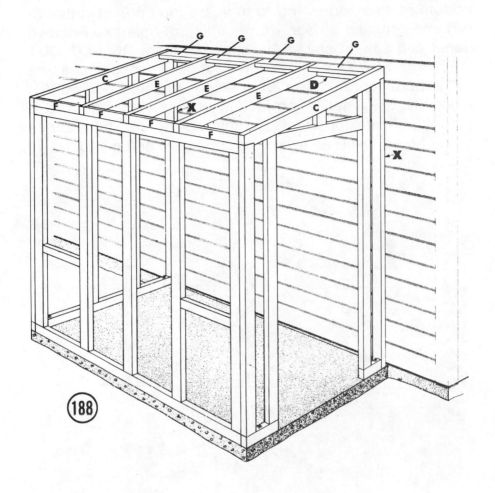

You can sheath kennel with ⅛ or 3/16″ hardboard, ¼″ exterior grade plywood or ⅜ or ½″ plyscord sheathing. If you plan on siding kennel with clapboard or shingles, ⅜ or ½″ plyscord sheathing can be used. After nailing to studs, cover plyscord with #15 felt. Staple felt horizontally. Start at bottom and overlap each horizontal strip 4 to 6″. If you want to sheath and paint kennel, ⅛ or 3/16″ hardboard or other exterior sheathing can be applied. Always read and follow manufacturer's directions and apply a primer where required before painting.

Temporarily butt and tack a 4 x 8 panel to end against building. Check outer edge with a level. With bottom flush with bottom of shoe, draw line to indicate top edge of rafter C. If frame contains a door, draw outline of opening. Remove panel and saw to shape and size required. DO NOT CUT OPENING FOR DOOR. If frame contains a door, measure ⅜″ in from door outline. Cut opening in panel 2′6¾ x 6′⅜″, Illus. 189, 190. The ⅜″ projection acts as a door stop. Use cutout to sheath door frame. To saw top corners, drill a series of ⅛″ holes. Insert a keyhole or saber saw and cut to drawn line.

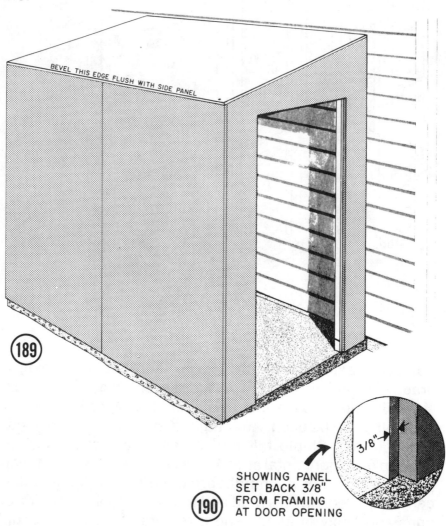

BEVEL THIS EDGE FLUSH WITH SIDE PANEL

(189)

(190) SHOWING PANEL SET BACK 3/8" FROM FRAMING AT DOOR OPENING

3/8"

Exterior weatherproof panel board should be nailed to studs with nails manufacturer specifies. After nailing first end panel, apply other end panel following same procedure, then cut side panel to size required. Cut openings in side panel for dog entry.

Side panels should butt together over stud. Plane top edge to match pitch of roof.

Cut roof panel to length required so it finishes flush with end and side panel, Illus. 189. Cut and nail extra strip of roof panel to fill gap.

If an outside door is to be installed, build frame, Illus. 191, to size shown or size required. Apply glue and fasten framing with two ⅝" corrugated fasteners in each joint.

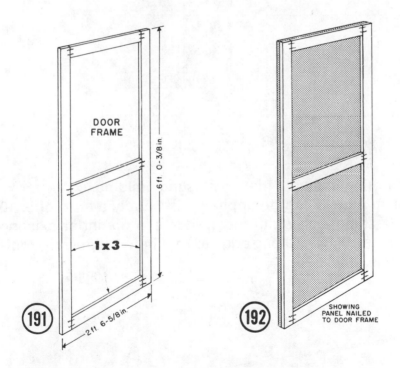

DOOR FRAME

6 ft 0-3/8 in.

1 x 3

191

2 ft 6-5/8 in.

192

SHOWING PANEL NAILED TO DOOR FRAME

After checking to make certain frame is square, apply glue and nail panel board to frame, Illus. 192.

If an outside door is installed, apply 1 x 3 door casing around opening, Illus. 193. Door can be hung with three 4″ T-hinges in position shown. A 3½″ door hasp, fastened in position shown, permits padlocking kennel door.

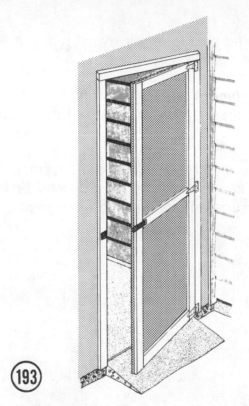

(193)

Apply roofing to match that on existing building, or V-groove aluminum panels can be applied. First apply a strip of 8, 10 or 12″ flashing, use width required to slip up under existing siding, Illus.194. Nail along edge to roof before applying roofing panels, Illus. 195.

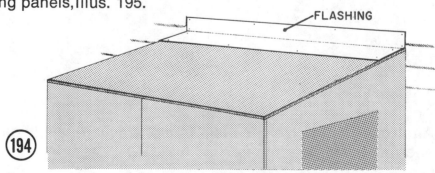

FLASHING

(194)

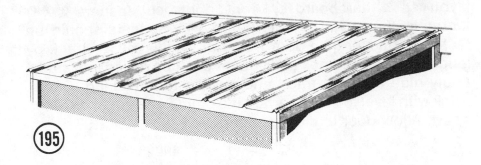

(195)

Sliding kennel doors can be installed as shown in Illus. 196. Use ³⁄₁₆″ tempered hardboard or ³⁄₈″ plywood for door. Cut door 2″ wider and taller than opening.

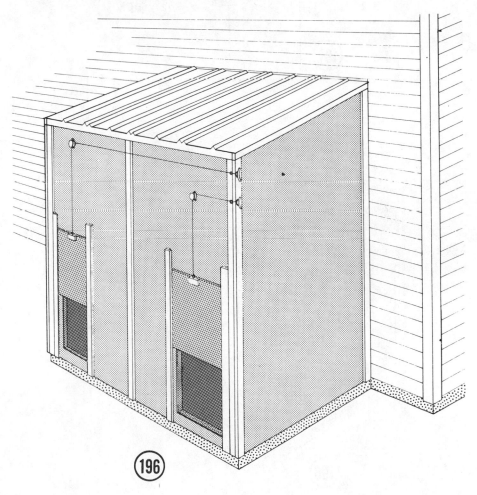

(196)

If you use ³⁄₁₆″ hardboard for kennel doors, cut spacers ³⁄₈ x ³⁄₄ x double the height of door, Illus. 197. Spacers should be ¹⁄₁₆ to ¹⁄₈″ thicker than door material. Cut ³⁄₈ x 1½″ track by length required. If track and spacer can't be nailed into studs, apply glue and bolt track and spacer to sheathing. Check track with level to make certain it's plumb and equal distance apart. Allow door to clear spacers ¼″, Illus. 198, 199.

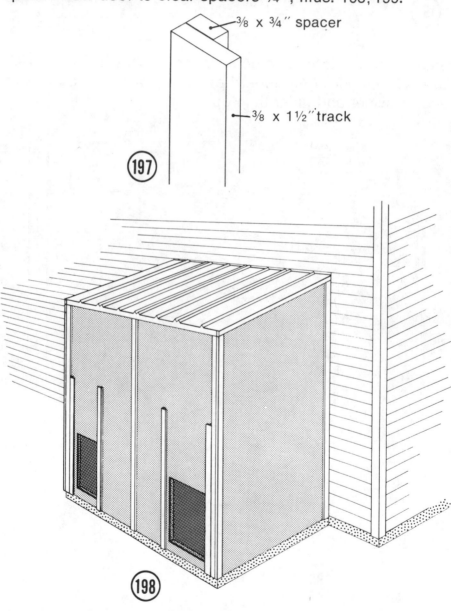

³⁄₈ x ³⁄₄″ spacer

³⁄₈ x 1½″ track

197

198

Apply glue and screw door panel to 1 x 2 x 4″ block. Fasten screw eye to block, Illus. 199. Sliding doors can be raised or lowered with a nylon cord through a block pulley and eye, Illus. 200. Fasten block pulley, eye and cleat in position shown, Illus. 196.

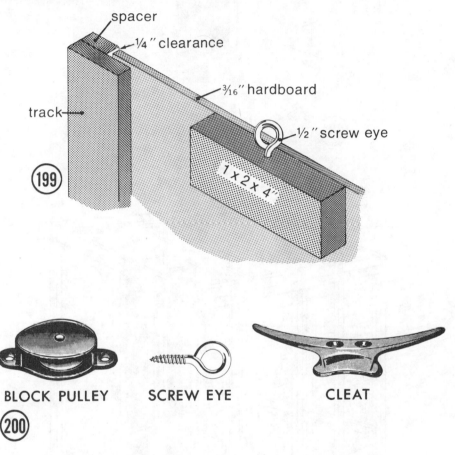

spacer
¼″ clearance
³⁄₁₆″ hardboard
track
½″ screw eye
1 x 2 x 4″
199

BLOCK PULLEY SCREW EYE CLEAT

200

Cut 30″ opening in garage, Illus. 201, when no outside door is used. This permits building a raised sleeping platform, Illus. 202. Size of bed depends on size of dog. It can range from 24 x 30″ to 36 x 48″. A sleeping shelf built over the entry keeps the dog out of a draft. In areas subject to cold winters, nail 2 x 4 framing on edge. Provide opening so dog can jump up on shelf. Nail ¼ or ⅜ plywood to bottom. Fill area with rock wool insulation, then nail ½ or ⅝″ plywood floor to framing, Illus. 203.

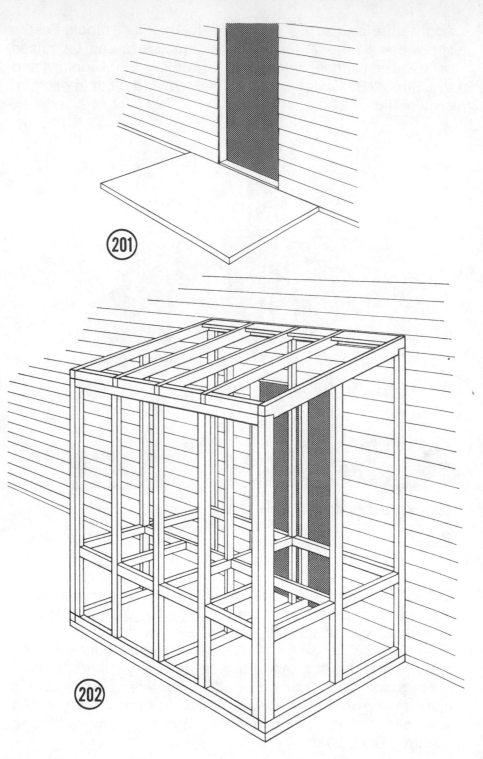

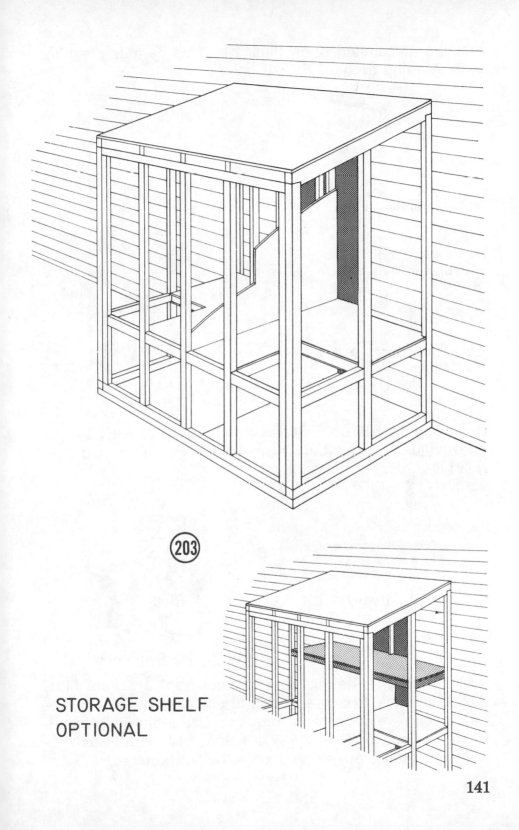

203

STORAGE SHELF
OPTIONAL

Install a 36″ sliding door, Illus. 204. This permits cleaning both sleeping areas.

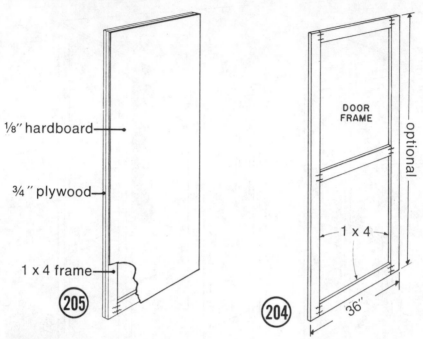

Build door 3′ x 6′8″ or 7′. Screw or nail 1 x 4 or 1 x 6 in position shown, Illus. 205. Your building materials retailer sells a trolley rail, Illus. 206.

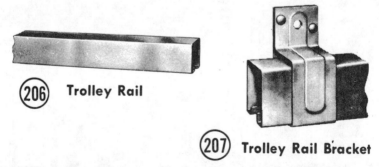

To install track at height required, slide track brackets, Illus. 207, over track. Space and bolt brackets every 24″, or distance apart weight of door requires. Use a bathroom scale to weigh door. Spike a 2 x 6 at height and length track requires. Fasten brackets to 2 x 6 at height required.

Mount door hangers, Illus. 208, 209, 3″ in from edge of door or distance from edge manufacturer of hardware suggests. NOTE: Head of bolt must be placed in position shown.

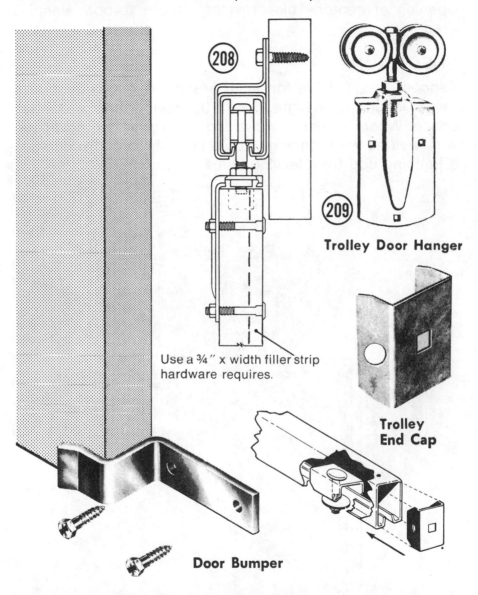

Trolley Door Hanger

Use a ¾″ x width filler strip hardware requires.

Trolley End Cap

Door Bumper

If door hardware requires a thicker door, cut ¼, ⅜, ½″ or thickness plywood to size required. Nail in position before attaching door hardware. Door hangers are adjustable and permit up to ½″ vertical adjustment.

143

If 4' or more of floor space, by length required, is available inside a garage, frame in a partition wall. Sheath partition with asbestos cement board, ⅜ or ½" plyscord. Frame a 36" opening at center. This provides access to both sleeping areas.

ERECT RUNS

Fenced runs, 3' wide for small breeds, 4' for medium size by 16' long, 4 to 6' high, Illus. 210, provide ample exercise space. Where valuable show dogs are boarded, cover run with welded wire fencing, Illus. 211. This also discourages a jumping dog from leaving home.

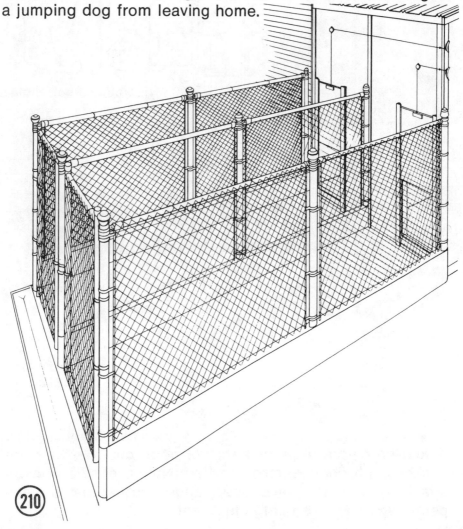

(210)

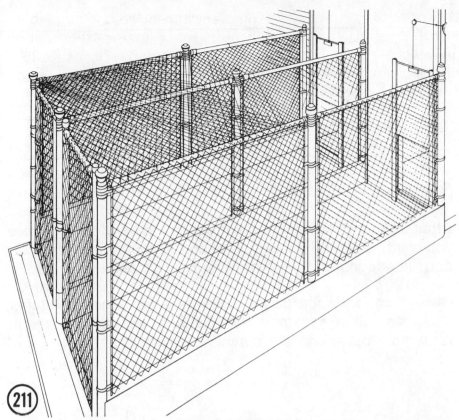

(211)

Small breeds, dogs weighing up to 40 lbs. can move freely in 3' wide runs. Police dogs and larger breeds, those weighing up to 100 lbs. frequently require a 5' wide run. St. Bernards need even more space. While a St. Bernard doesn't do much running, he does need to move around. This size dog should have a 6' wide exercise area.

For sanitary reasons, outside runs must comply with either the local building or Board of Health codes. While 1½" of concrete over a 2" bed of gravel is ample, as is 2" of asphalt, a local code may specify a thicker slab.

After selecting site for run, set up stakes and run guide lines. Depending on space available, 16' runs are ideal for the larger breeds, while a 12' run is ample for the smaller dogs. Stake out 3', 4' to 6' wide runs. Check diagonals to make certain each run is square, Illus. 212.

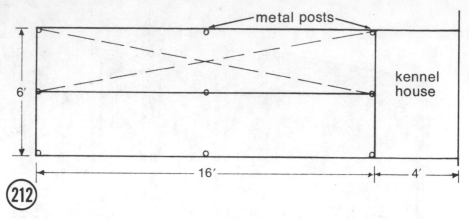

metal posts

kennel house

6'

16'

4'

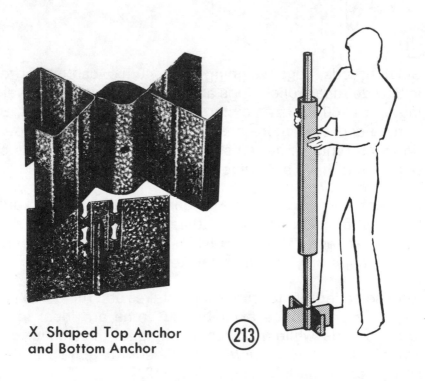

After staking out space for kennel and runs, decide where you want water and lighting. Use underground cable for outdoor floodlighting. Bury waterline below frost level.

Always space fence posts distance apart fencing retailer suggests. Drive posts in line and in position at height required. Post anchors are available, Illus. 213.

X Shaped Top Anchor and Bottom Anchor

213

146

Plan on pouring an 1½ x 9¼" high curb between runs for medium size breeds, Illus. 214; an 1½ x 15½" curb for the larger breeds. Excavate to a depth below frost level. Use 2 x 10 x 16' for forms. Curbs should follow same pitch as run. Nail 2 x 10 to stakes. Slope form 4" in 16'.

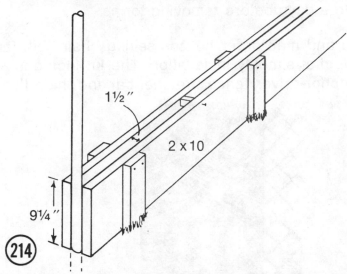

1½"

2 x 10

9¼"

214

Use 1 x 2 separators to hold forms plumb and exact distance apart, Illus. 214. Drive nails only part way into ends. This simplifies withdrawing separator after you start filling, without disturbing the form.

Cut 6 x 6 reinforcing wire to length required. Position in center of form, Illus. 215.

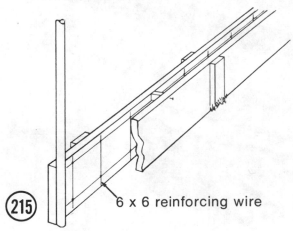

215 6 x 6 reinforcing wire

Pour curb using concrete consisting of 1 part cement, 3 parts sand to 5 parts small gravel, or buy readymix. Use a wet mix so form can be filled without air pockets. Check each post with a level in two directions as you pour the curb. Be sure to anchor corner posts with sufficient concrete. Allow curbs to set three days before removing forms.

Retailers and mail order houses selling chain link fencing rent tools that simplify installation. The kit includes a post driver, anchor-driver, fence stretcher bar and chain, Illus. 216, 217.

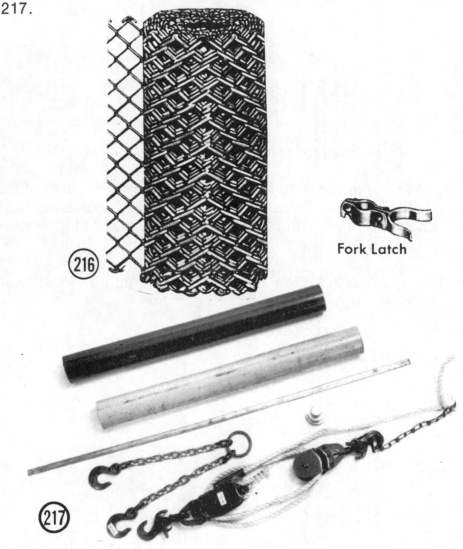

Fork Latch

You can either level up area of a run with 2″ of gravel, or excavate to permit spreading gravel to height needed. To simplify laying 1½″ of concrete with ¼″ per foot slope, lay 2 x 4 x 16′, or length required, flatwise alongside the curbs, Illus. 218. Raise end near kennel 4″ for a 16′ run. Use globs of concrete to position form to slope desired. Use a straight 2 x 4 by slightly less than width between curbs, and a level, to make certain both forms are level across.

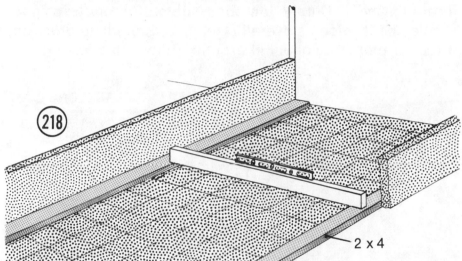

2 x 4

Pour one half of overall thickness required. Cut 6 x 6 wire to width required and embed in wet cement. Pour balance of concrete equal to top of form. Screed concrete with a 2 x 4, Illus. 172, level with form. For a smooth finish, use a float, Illus. 174. Allow concrete to begin to set, then remove forms and fill void with concrete. Trowel smooth.

Recommended Septic Tank Capacities

Required total tank capacity in gallons	Tank Size			
	Inside width	Inside length	Liquid depth	Total depth
750	3 ft. 6 in.	7 ft. 6 in.	4 ft. 0 in.	5 ft. 0 in.
900	3 ft. 6 in.	8 ft. 0 in.	4 ft. 6 in.	5 ft. 6 in.
1,000	4 ft. 0 in.	8 ft. 0 in.	4 ft. 6 in.	5 ft. 6 in.
1,250	4 ft. 0 in.	9 ft. 0 in.	4 ft. 6 in.	5 ft. 6 in.

Runs that slope ¼″ to a foot from kennel simplify hosing. A commercial kennel usually necessitates installation of a septic tank and field. The Board of Health will specify size, Illus. 219. You can build this by following directions outlined in Book #632.

A 55 gallon steel drum can be used as a septic tank for a small private kennel. Drill or punch ½ or ¾″ holes to perforate the sides. Cut the top and bottom off drum. Excavate a hole about twice its overall size, Illus. 220. Place drum on a foot or more of stone. Fill around drum with stone.

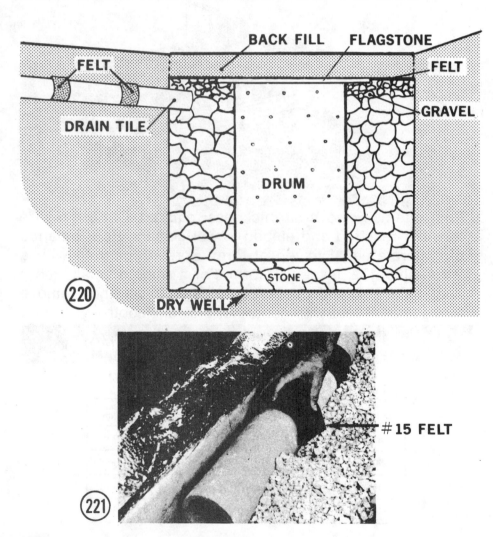

BACK FILL   FLAGSTONE

FELT   FELT

                                                 GRAVEL
DRAIN TILE

DRUM

STONE
(220)
DRY WELL

(221)   #15 FELT

Slope a 4″ drain from end of gutter to top of drum. Wrap joints between drain pipe with #15 felt, Illus. 221. Lay stone to height equal to or above drum. Place a slate or flagstone on top. Cover flagstone and stone with #15 felt and carefully backfill.

Allow runs to set three days before fastening fencing to posts.

Homeowners who want to partition off part of a garage for a kennel, can frequently do so without applying for a permit. First talk this over with your neighbors so none will complain about your "disturbing the peace," Illus. 222.

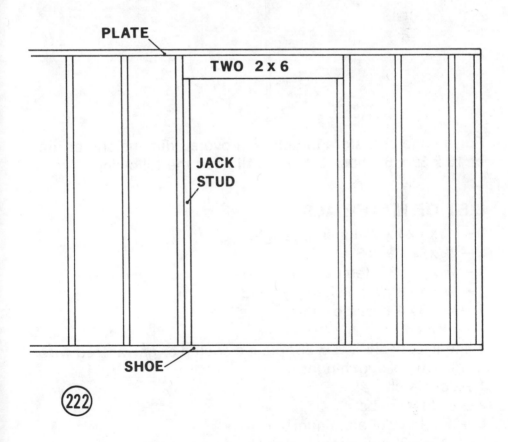

PLATE

TWO 2 x 6

JACK
STUD

SHOE

222

PARAKEET CAGE

Everyone exposed to the charm, conversation and magnetic waves of affection that emanate from a pair of parakeets, finds the critters irresistibly fascinating. Recognizing this appeal, directions explain how to build a cage and storage unit that will easily accommodate two or more pairs. Each pair requires a nest, Illus. 223. Those who decide to go into quantity production can lengthen the cage to six or eight feet.

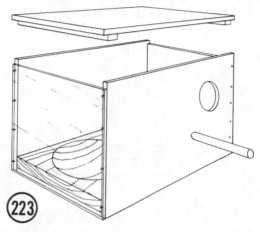

For a cage and storage unit with overall dimensions at top of 16 x 32 x 6', Illus. 224, you will need the following:

LIST OF MATERIALS

9 — ¹⁄₁₆ x 1 x 1 x 6' aluminum angle
2 — ¹⁄₁₆ x ¾ x ¾ x 6'   "   "
1 — ⅛ x 16 x 32" tempered hardboard
1 — ¼ x 4 x 8' prefinished plywood
1 — ½ x 3 x 4' particle board
2 — 1 x 2 x 8'
8 lineal feet — ½ x ½ x 36" plastic coated or galvanized wire
2 prs. cabinet door hinges
1 — door latch
2 — 1" door knobs
5 — ⅛ x ¾ x 8'0" aluminum bar stock
1 pr. 1½ x 2" stainless steel or aluminum hinges
1 tray handle

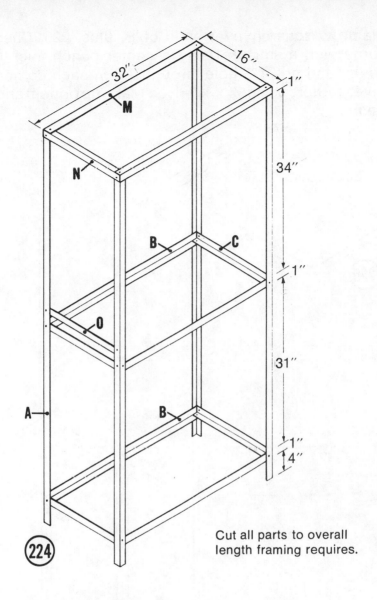

32″

16″

1″

M

N

34″

B   C

1″

O

31″

A

B

1″
4″

Cut all parts to overall
length framing requires.

(224)

Use ⅟₁₆ x 1 x 1″ aluminum angle for parts A, B, C, M, N, O. You will need four 6′ for A. Cut four B — 31¾″; four C — 15¾″; two M — 32″; two N — 15⅞″; one O — 15¾″. Since the top frame covers outside face of legs A, while the middle and bottom frame butts against the inside, the overall size of cabinet measures 15⅞ x 31⅞″ at floor. Always check inner framing dimensions before cutting. This eliminates error and simplifies cutting to size your construction requires.

Clamp C squarely over ends of B, Illus. 225. Check each corner wth a square. Using a center punch, nick metal in center and drill ⅛″ hole through AB in each corner. "Pop" Rivet corners using ⅛ x ⅜″ rivet. Make up bottom and middle frame.

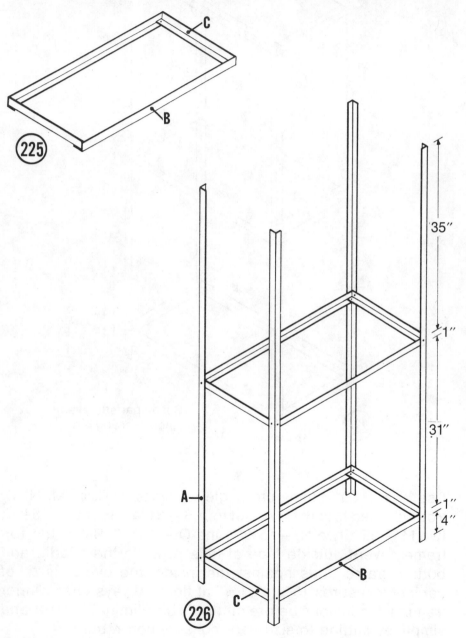

154

Drill holes and "Pop" Rivet legs A to bottom frame, 4" and 36", Illus. 226.

Cut ¼" prefinished plywood back 31⅝ x 31⅞", Illus. 227. Apply glue and brad back panel to a ¾ x ¾ x 29⅝" strip. Position strip 1" from ends and flush with top and bottom edge.

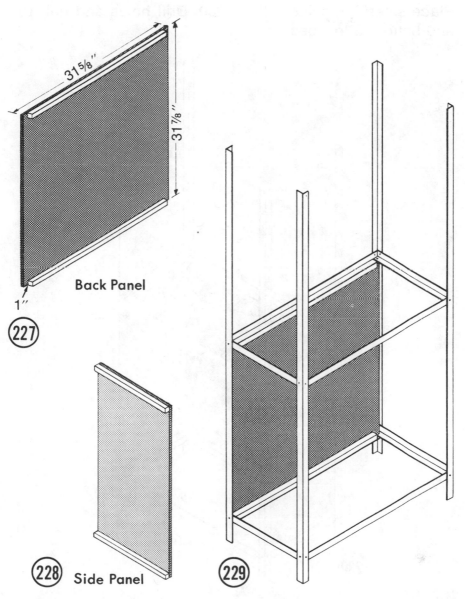

31⅝"

31⅞"

Back Panel

1"

227

228 **Side Panel**

229

Cut two ¼″ prefinished plywood sides, Illus. 228, 15½ x 31⅞″. Glue and brad sides to ¾ x ¾ x 15½″ strips in position shown.

Place back in position, Illus. 229. Drill four ⅛″ holes through top and bottom B. Brad B to wood strips with 1″ aluminum nails.

Place sides in position, Illus. 230. Drill holes and nail top and bottom C to sides.

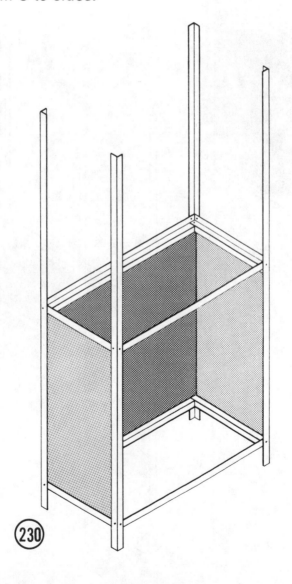

230

Cut ¼" prefinished plywood 15⅝ x 31⅝" for bottom shelf, or to size framing requires. With good face down, glue a ¾ x ¾ x 29⅝" strip flush with front edge. Turn panel over and drive brads through panel into strip, Illus. 231. Apply glue to strips on back and sides. Brad floor to wood strips with finished face up.

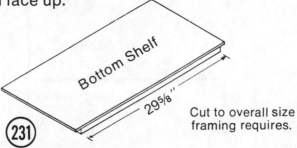

Bottom Shelf

29⅝"

Cut to overall size framing requires.

(231)

Make up a 1 x 2 frame, Illus. 232, 15½ x 31½" or to size middle shelf requires, less amount required for ½ x ½" wire mesh.

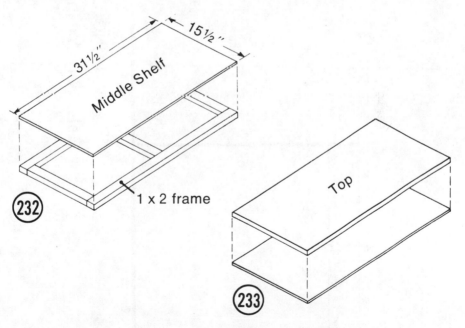

31½"

15½"

Middle Shelf

1 x 2 frame

(232)

Top

(233)

Make up top, Illus. 233. Use ¼" prefinished plywood and ½" particle board. Keeping finished face of ¼" plywood facing down, glue and brad panel to ½" particle board.

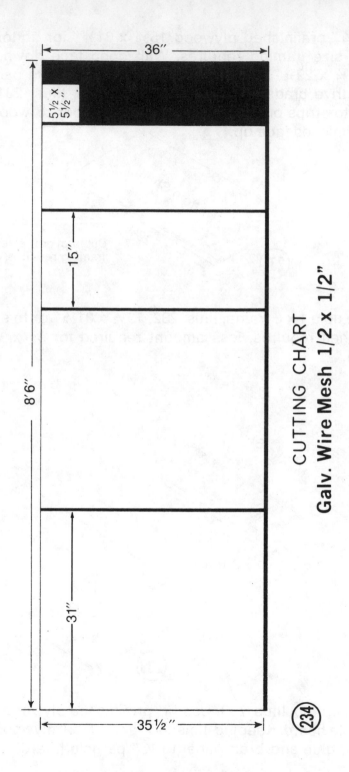

36"

5½ x
5½ "

15"

8'6"

31"

CUTTING CHART
Galv. Wire Mesh 1/2 x 1/2"

35½ "

(234)

158

Cut ½ x ½″ galvanized or aluminum wire to size shown, Illus. 234, or to size framing requires. Always cut on outside of a strand to keep pigtails as short as possible.

Staple wire to top and middle shelf, Illus. 235.

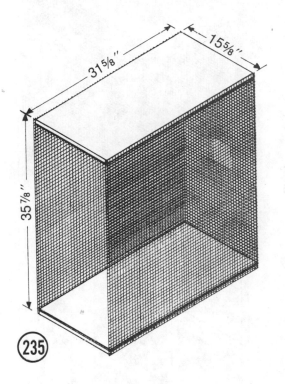

Lay assembled frame on floor, Illus. 236, and slide assembled cage in place. Use care not to bend wire.

Drill ⅛″ holes through C. Nail C to middle shelf with 1″ aluminum nails.

Check overall size for 1 x 1 top frame MN. This goes on outside of A, Illus. 237. Cut two M — 32″; two N — 15⅞″; or cut MN to length required. "Pop" Rivet together, Illus. 225. Place frame in position. Drill holes and nail MN to ½″ panel. Cut 1/16 x ¾ x ¾″ angle 36″ or length required. Drill holes and "Pop" Rivet angle to A in each corner, Illus. 237A.

159

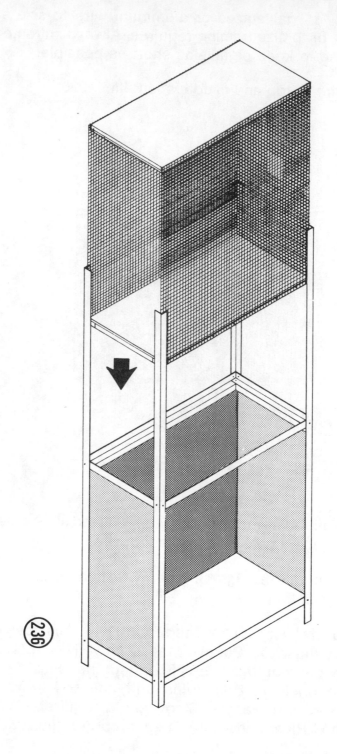

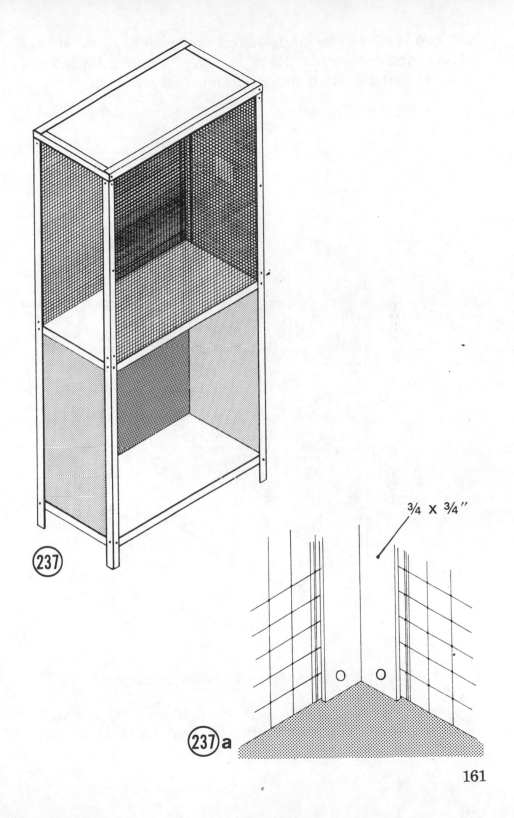

237

237a

¾ x ¾″

Cut two ½ x 2½" x length required and two ¼ x 2½" strips of plywood for corner posts in lower cabinet, Illus. 238. Use ½" particle board and ¼" prefinished plywood.

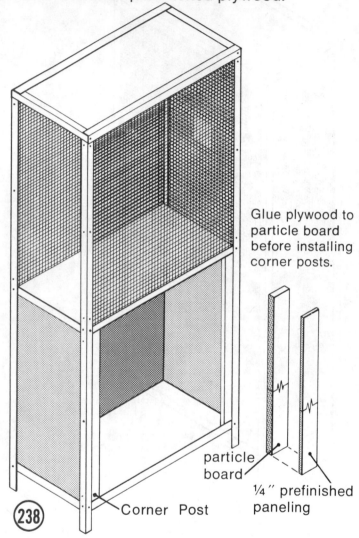

Glue plywood to particle board before installing corner posts.

particle board

¼" prefinished paneling

Corner Post

(238)

Drill holes through framing and nail in position.

Cut two side cleats, one back cleat, Illus. 239, to length required. Apply glue and brad back and sides to cleats. Install shelf. Shelf acts as a door stop.

162

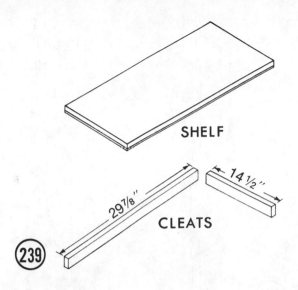

SHELF

29⅞″

14½″

CLEATS

(239)

Assemble two cabinet doors, Illus. 240, to size opening requires. Use ½″ particle board and ¼″ prefinished paneling. Glue prefinished plywood to particle board. Place assembled doors on a flat surface. Apply weight. Allow glue to set.

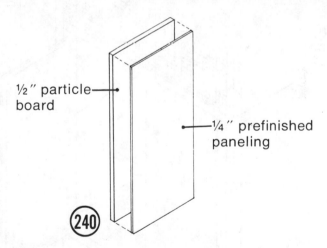

½″ particle board

¼″ prefinished paneling

(240)

Fasten hinges 2½″ from bottom and top of door. Mortise edge of door to receive hinge, Illus. 241. Screw hinge in place. Door catches can be fastened to door and to bottom of shelf, Illus. 242. Drill holes and fasten 1″ door knob to each door.

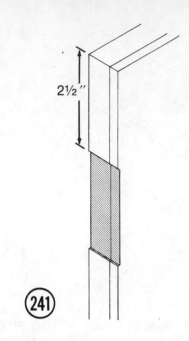

2½″

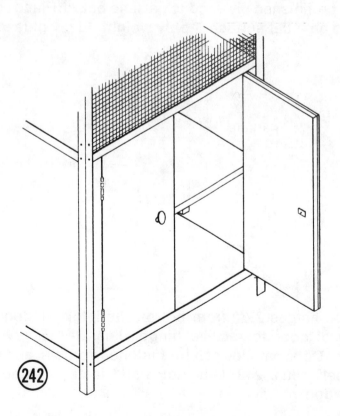

Allow slot for litter tray. "Pop" Rivet ⅟₁₆ x 1 x 1 x 15¾" O in position shown, Illus. 243.

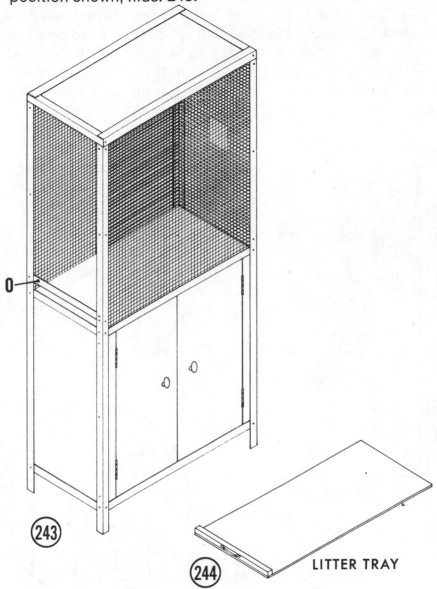

LITTER TRAY

Cut ⅛" tempered hardboard 13¾ x 31¼" for a litter tray. Cut a ¾ x ¾ x 13½" block. Glue and brad hardboard to block, Illus. 244. Fasten a handle to edge. Cover hardboard with a sanded sheet of paper sold by most pet stores. Use it for litter removal.

Build a frame to overall size open end requires less ¼″ in width and length. This allows ⅛″ clearance all around. Use ⅛ x ¾″ bar stock and ½ x ½″ wire. "Pop" Rivet frame together, Illus. 245, following same procedure outlined on page 61. Hang this door with a pair of 2 x 2″ hinges. Drill holes in A. "Pop Rivet hinge in position. Cut an 1½″ strip of ⅛ x ¾″ bar stock for latch stops, Illus. 245. Round ends with a file. "Pop" Rivet ¾ x ½″ stop in position noted.

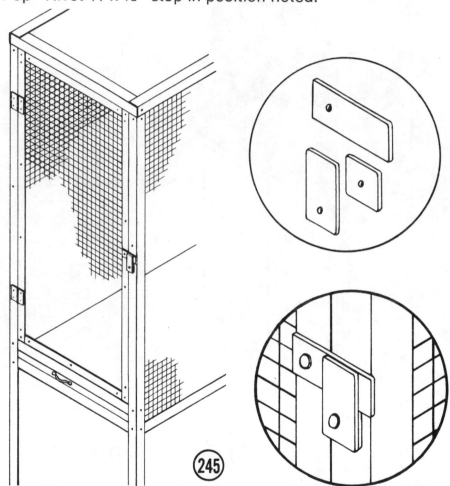

(245)

Use this door to install or remove nests. Cut a smaller opening, 4¾ x 4¾″, Illus. 246, or one not larger than your hand when holding a feed or water container, in center of one or both ends. File all wire ends around opening. Frame edge of opening, with sheet aluminum. Cut aluminum 6¼ x 6¼″. Cut an opening 3¼ x 3¼". Miter cut corners ¾". Bend lips. Insert in position. Fold and fasten lips down using pliers.

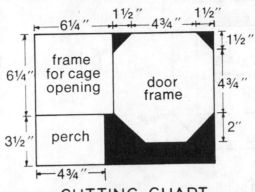

CUTTING CHART
sheet aluminum

.....Indicates fold lines

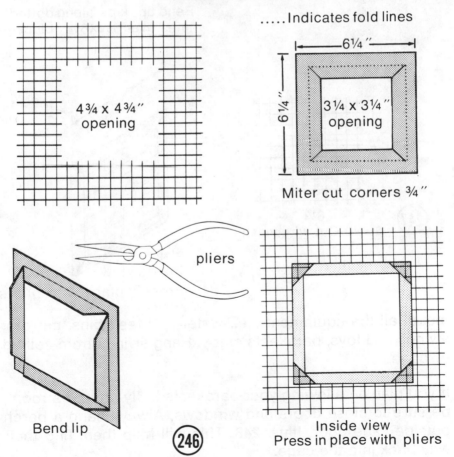

4¾ x 4¾" opening

6¼"

6¼"

3¼ x 3¼" opening

Miter cut corners ¾"

pliers

Bend lip

Inside view
Press in place with pliers

(246)

Make 6¼ x 6¼" wire door, Illus. 247. Hinge door with wire hooks.

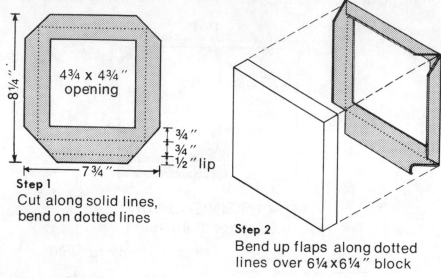

4¾ x 4¾" opening

8¼"

7¾"

¾"
¾"
½" lip

Step 1
Cut along solid lines, bend on dotted lines

Step 2
Bend up flaps along dotted lines over 6¼ x 6¼" block

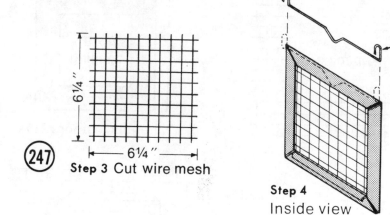

6¼"

6¼"

(247) **Step 3** Cut wire mesh

10" #14 galv. wire

Step 4
Inside view
Press in place with pliers

Install all the equipment, i.e., water and feed bins, mirrors, swings and toys, parakeets enjoy. Hang swings from ceiling of cage.

If you plan on allowing your parakeets to fly around a room, be sure to close doors and windows. Always hang a perch outside cage door, Illus. 248. This will help them find their way back into the cage.

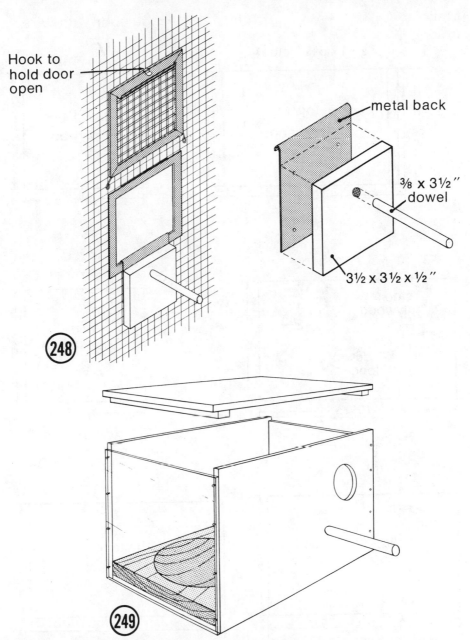

Hook to
hold door
open

metal back

⅜ x 3½"
dowel

3½ x 3½ x ½"

(248)

(249)

Build and install a box nest, Illus. 249, for each pair of para-keets. Cut parts from ⅜" plywood to size shown, Illus. 250. Cut a 2" hole in one side or end of nest box. Make a "bed" out of a 5½ x 9½" block, Illus. 251. Use 2 x 6. To scoop out a 5 to 5½" round, ½" deep concave bed, use a 5" disk sander.

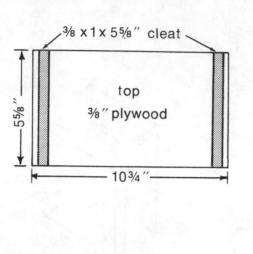

3/8 x 1 x 5 5/8″ cleat

top
3/8″ plywood

5 5/8″

10 3/4″

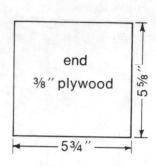

end
3/8″ plywood

5 5/8″

5 3/4″

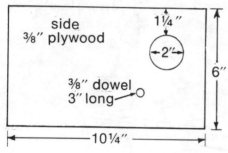

side
3/8″ plywood

1 1/4″

2″

3/8″ dowel
3″ long

6″

10 1/4″

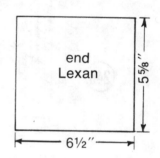

end
Lexan

5 5/8″

6 1/2″

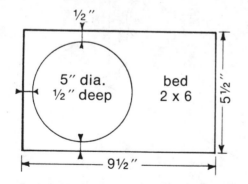

1/2″

5″ dia.
1/2″ deep

bed
2 x 6

5 1/2″

9 1/2″

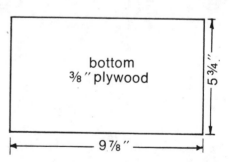

bottom
3/8″ plywood

5 3/4″

9 7/8″

NEST CUTTING CHART

250

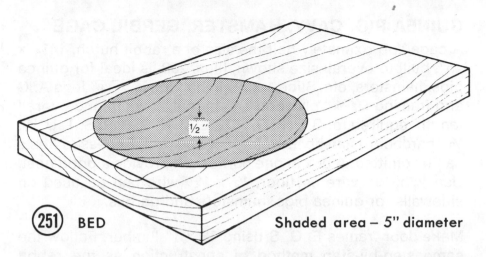

(251) BED   Shaded area – 5" diameter

Nail sides to bottom and ⅜" plywood end. If you want to see if a female has any eggs, nail a piece of Lexan instead of plywood to one end. Place this end against cage. Cover outside of cage with a ¼" panel to keep out the light. Drill a ⅜" hole and insert a 3" piece of dowel in position shown.

Place completed cage in a draft free room. Cover at night.

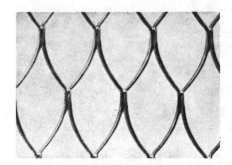

Gold Panorama Pattern
may be used in place of ½ x ½" wire mesh.

GUINEA PIG, CAVY, HAMSTER, GERBIL CAGE

A cage approximately half the size of a rabbit hutch, 14¼ x 45", built to overall size shown, Illus. 252, is ideal for guinea pigs, hamsters, etc. Slice 1 x 2's in half for ¾ x ¾" legs A, C and framing D. ⅜" plywood can be cut to width and overall length required for B, E, F, G, H, K, L, M, N, O, P, R, S, T, U, W. ⅛" hardboard can be used for V, X and roof. Recessed nests can be omitted. A box in one corner will provide a good nest. Use ¼ x ¼" wire on floor, ½ x ½" wire can be used on sidewalls for guinea pigs, hamsters and gerbils.

Make door frames E, G, S using ¾ x 1" lumber. Follow the same step-by-step method of construction as the rabbit hutch.

SIZE OF PARTS

4 — ¾ x ¾ x 27⅛" — A
4 — ⅜ x 1¾ x 45" — B
4 — ¾ x ¾ x 30" — C
2 — ¾ x ¾ x 13⅝" — D
2 — ⅜ x ¾ x 7⅜" — E
1 — ⅜ x 7⅜ x 7" — F
4 — ⅜ x ¾ x 10" — G
4 — ⅜ x 1¾ x 2⅜" — H
4 — ⅜ x 1¾ x 11¼" — K
2 — ⅜ x 1¾ x 45" — L
2 — ⅜ x 1¾ x 19⅜" — M
1 — ⅜ x 1¾ x 4¾" — N
2 — ⅜ x 1¾ x 6¼" — O
2 — ⅜ x 1⅞ x 4⅜ x 12⅜" — P
2 — ⅜ x 1⅝ x 45⅝ x 14¼" — R
4 — ⅜ x ¾ x 7⅜" — S
2 — ⅜ x 1¾ x 14¼" — T
2 — ⅜ x ⅜ x 5¾" — U
1 — ⅛ x 8⅝ x 11⅞ x 11" — V
2 — ⅜ x ¾ x 2¼ x 4½" — W
2 — ⅛ x 4¾ x 12" — X
1 — ⅜ x 1¾ x 5½" — Y

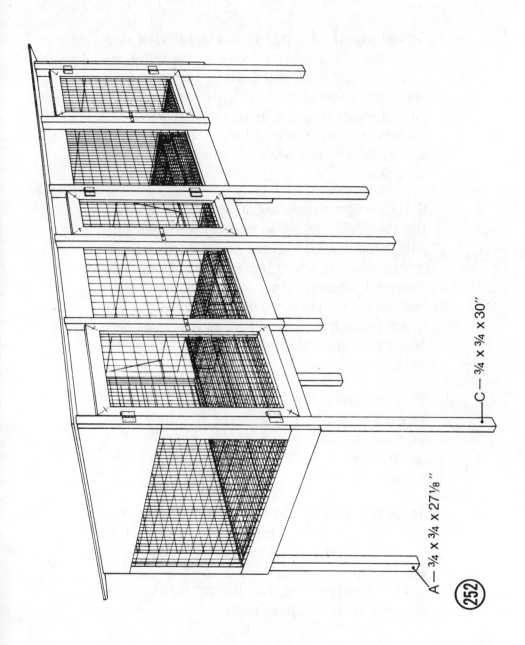

A — ¾ x ¾ x 27⅛"

C — ¾ x ¾ x 30"

252

173

HOW TO THINK METRIC

Government officials concerned with the adoption of the metric system are quick to warn anyone from attempting to make precise conversions. One quickly accepts this advice when they begin to convert yards to meters or vice versa. Place a metric ruler alongside a foot ruler and you get the message fast.

Since a meter equals 1.09361 yards, or 39⅜" +, the decimals can drive you up a creek. The government men suggest accepting a rough, rather than an exact equivalent. They recommend considering a meter in the same way you presently use a yard. A kilometer as 0.6 of a mile. A kilogram or kilo as just over two pounds. A liter, a quart, with a small extra swig.

To more fully appreciate why a rough conversion is preferable, note the 6" rule alongside the metric rule. A meter contains 100 centimeters. A centimeter contains 10 millimeters.

As an introduction to the metric system, we used a metric rule to measure standard U.S. building materials. Since a 1x2 measures anywheres from ¾ to ²⁵⁄₃₂ x 1½", which is typical of U.S. lumber sizes, the metric equivalents shown are only approximate.

Consider 1" equal to 2.54 centimeters;
10" = 25.4 cm.
To multiply 4¼" into centimeters: 4.25 × 2.54 = 10.795 or 10.8 cm.

EASY-TO-USE-METRIC SCALE

DECIMAL EQUIVALENTS

Fraction	Decimal
1/32	.03125
1/16	.0625
3/32	.09375
1/8	.125
5/32	.15625
3/16	.1875
7/32	.21875
1/4	.250
9/32	.28125
5/16	.3125
11/32	.34375
3/8	.375
13/32	.40625
7/16	.4375
15/32	.46875
1/2	.500
17/32	.53125
9/16	.5625
19/32	.59375
5/8	.625
21/32	.65625
11/16	.6875
23/32	.71875
3/4	.750
25/32	.78125
13/16	.8125
27/32	.84375
7/8	.875
29/32	.90625
15/16	.9375
31/32	.96875

FRACTIONS — CENTIMETERS

Fraction	Centimeters
1/16	0.16
1/8	0.32
3/16	0.48
1/4	0.64
5/16	0.79
3/8	0.95
7/16	1.11
1/2	1.27
9/16	1.43
5/8	1.59
11/16	1.75
3/4	1.91
13/16	2.06
7/8	2.22
15/16	2.38

INCHES — CENTIMETERS

Inches	Centimeters
1	2.54
1/8	2.9
1/4	3.2
3/8	3.5
1/2	3.8
5/8	4.1
3/4	4.4
7/8	4.8
2	5.1
1/8	5.4
1/4	5.7
3/8	6.0
1/2	6.4
5/8	6.7
3/4	7.0
7/8	7.3
3	7.6
1/8	7.9
1/4	8.3
3/8	8.6
1/2	8.9
5/8	9.2
3/4	9.5
7/8	9.8
4	10.2
1/8	10.5
1/4	10.8
3/8	11.1
1/2	11.4
5/8	11.7
3/4	12.1
7/8	12.4
5	12.7
1/8	13.0
1/4	13.3
3/8	13.7
1/2	14.0
5/8	14.3
3/4	14.6
7/8	14.9

6		15.2
1/8		15.6
	1/4	15.9
3/8		16.2
	1/2	16.5
5/8		16.8
	3/4	17.1
7/8		17.5
7		17.8
1/8		18.1
	1/4	18.4
3/8		18.7
	1/2	19.1
5/8		19.4
	3/4	19.7
7/8		20.0
8		20.3
1/8		20.6
	1/4	21.0
3/8		21.3
	1/2	21.6
5/8		21.9
	3/4	22.2
7/8		22.5
9		22.9
1/8		23.2
	1/4	23.5
3/8		23.8
	1/2	24.1
5/8		24.4
	3/4	24.8
7/8		25.1
10		25.4
1/8		25.7
	1/4	26.0
3/8		26.4
	1/2	26.7
5/8		27.0
	3/4	27.3
7/8		27.6
11		27.9
1/8		28.3
	1/4	28.6
3/8		28.9
	1/2	29.2
5/8		29.5
	3/4	29.8
7/8		30.2

12		30.5
1/8		30.8
	1/4	31.1
3/8		31.4
	1/2	31.8
5/8		32.1
	3/4	32.4
7/8		32.7
14		35.6
16		40.6
20		50.8
30		76.2
40		101.6
50		127.0
60		152.4
70		177.8
80		203.2
90		228.6
100		254.0

FEET	INCHES	CENTIMETERS
1	12	30.5
2	24	61.0
3	36	91.4
4	48	121.9
5	60	152.4
6	72	182.9
7	84	213.4
8	96	243.8
9	108	274.3
10	120	304.8
11	132	335.3
12	144	365.8
13	156	396.2
14	168	426.7
15	180	457.2
16	192	487.7
17	204	518.2
18	216	548.6
19	228	579.1
20	240	609.6

HANDY - REFERENCE - LUMBER
PLYWOOD - FLAKEBOARD - HARDBOARD - MOLDINGS

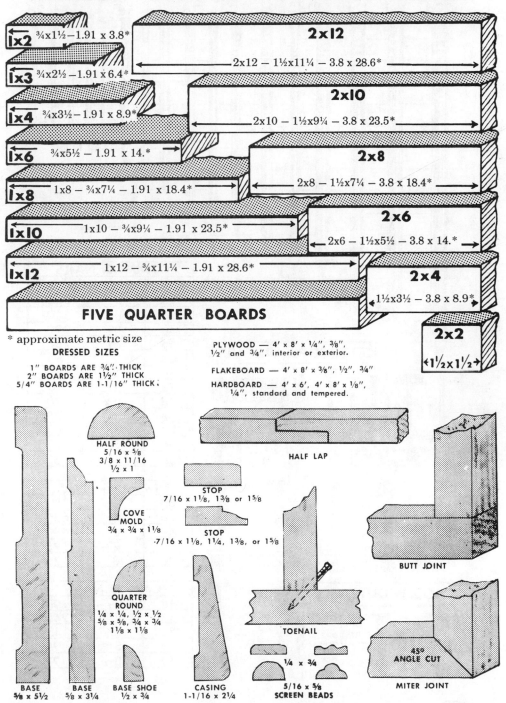

1x2 ¾x1½ – 1.91 x 3.8*

2x12
2x12 – 1½x11¼ – 3.8 x 28.6*

1x3 ¾x2½ – 1.91 x 6.4*

2x10
2x10 – 1½x9¼ – 3.8 x 23.5*

1x4 ¾x3½ – 1.91 x 8.9*

1x6 ¾x5½ – 1.91 x 14.*

2x8
2x8 – 1½x7¼ – 3.8 x 18.4*

1x8 1x8 – ¾x7¼ – 1.91 x 18.4*

2x6
2x6 – 1½x5½ – 3.8 x 14.*

1x10 1x10 – ¾x9¼ – 1.91 x 23.5*

1x12 1x12 – ¾x11¼ – 1.91 x 28.6*

2x4
1½x3½ – 3.8 x 8.9*

FIVE QUARTER BOARDS

2x2
1½x1½

* approximate metric size

DRESSED SIZES

1" BOARDS ARE ¾" THICK
2" BOARDS ARE 1½" THICK
5/4" BOARDS ARE 1-1/16" THICK

PLYWOOD — 4' x 8' x ¼", ⅜", ½" and ¾", interior or exterior.

FLAKEBOARD — 4' x 8' x ⅜", ½", ¾"

HARDBOARD — 4' x 6', 4' x 8' x ⅛", ¼", standard and tempered.

HALF ROUND
5/16 x ⅝
3/8 x 11/16
½ x 1

HALF LAP

STOP
7/16 x 1⅛, 1⅜ or 1⅝

COVE MOLD
¾ x ¾ x 1⅛

STOP
7/16 x 1⅛, 1¼, 1⅜, or 1⅝

BUTT JOINT

QUARTER ROUND
¼ x ¼, ½ x ½
⅝ x ⅝, ¾ x ¾
1⅛ x 1⅛

TOENAIL

45º ANGLE CUT

BASE
⅝ x 5½

BASE
⅝ x 3¼

BASE SHOE
½ x ¾

CASING
1-1/16 x 2¼

¼ x ¾

5/16 x ⅝
SCREEN BEADS

MITER JOINT

HANDY REFERENCE-NAILS
Common— Finishing—

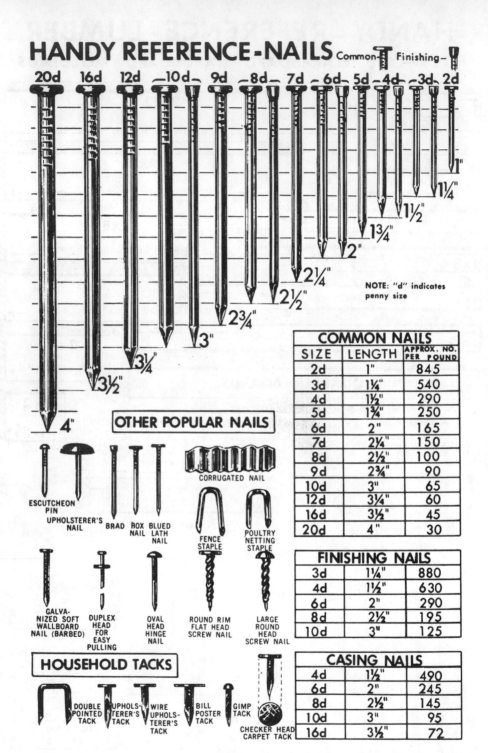

NOTE: "d" indicates penny size

OTHER POPULAR NAILS

ESCUTCHEON PIN
UPHOLSTERER'S NAIL
BRAD
BOX NAIL
BLUED LATH NAIL
CORRUGATED NAIL
FENCE STAPLE
POULTRY NETTING STAPLE

GALVANIZED SOFT WALLBOARD NAIL (BARBED)
DUPLEX HEAD FOR EASY PULLING
OVAL HEAD HINGE NAIL
ROUND RIM FLAT HEAD SCREW NAIL
LARGE ROUND HEAD SCREW NAIL

HOUSEHOLD TACKS

DOUBLE POINTED TACK
UPHOLSTERER'S TACK
WIRE UPHOLSTERER'S TACK
BILL POSTER TACK
GIMP TACK
CHECKER HEAD CARPET TACK

COMMON NAILS

SIZE	LENGTH	APPROX. NO. PER POUND
2d	1"	845
3d	1¼"	540
4d	1½"	290
5d	1¾"	250
6d	2"	165
7d	2¼"	150
8d	2½"	100
9d	2¾"	90
10d	3"	65
12d	3¼"	60
16d	3½"	45
20d	4"	30

FINISHING NAILS

3d	1¼"	880
4d	1½"	630
6d	2"	290
8d	2½"	195
10d	3"	125

CASING NAILS

4d	1½"	490
6d	2"	245
8d	2½"	145
10d	3"	95
16d	3½"	72